PLEASE UNDERESTIMATE ME

Jay Flewelling

Copyright © 2017 Jay Flewelling

This publication is protected under the US Copyright Act of 1976 and all other applicable international, federal, state and local laws, and all rights are reserved, including resale rights. No part of this publication may be reproduced, distributed, or transmitted in any form or by any means, including photocopying, recording, or other electronic or mechanical methods, without the prior written permission of the author, except in the case of brief quotations embodied in critical reviews and certain other noncommercial uses permitted by copyright law. For permission requests, write to the author at www.jayflewelling.com

Any trademarks, service marks, product names, or named features are assumed to be the property of their respective owners and are used only for reference. There is no implied endorsement if we used one of those terms.

Edited by Krysta Drechsler at The Red Pen (www.redpenpdx.com)

Cover Artwork by Jason Edward Davis

Cover Graphic Design by Jake Trudell

Cover Photography by Andy Batt

ISBN: 0-9994052-1-7
ISBN-13: 978-0-9994052-1-5

CONTENTS

Introduction	1
Volunteer Victim	5
Meth Jogger	8
Bad Tipper	10
Ambulances	14
Smokers are So Selfish	17
Italian Dinner	20
Smelli Carelli	25
Love. Proud.	30
In the Beginning	37
Sticker N' Plate	41
Wishful Gibberish	42
5-Day Clubs	46
The Bible	50
Betty Shover	53
Gilbert Blythe	55
60/40	59
Father-Son Embarrassment	63
Mortified	65
Jay's Story	71
Coming Out	74

PLEASE UNDERESTIMATE ME

Tina is a Bonch	78
Soccer Story	80
Lamy Amy Fabee	83
Nikay	87
Ribbon Racks	92
Work Schmerk	98
When Worlds Collide	116
Hamburger-Eating Champion	118
Push N' Shove	121
Naked Jay	124
To Everyone I Spam	129
Poop	131
Mountain Lake Jake	139
Thank You (Conclusion)	143

INTRODUCTION

I love when I am underestimated. Please think that you beat me. Please size me up as less than you. Please assume I will quit. Please assume that you will prevail, and I will be the doormat. You don't know me. You may think you know me. You may think you got me completely figured out and I am nothing. That is fine; please think of me as nothing. Please look at me with disgust or disdain. Because when I win (and I will win), it will make it that much better for me.

I have been underestimated my whole life—and it has made me a stronger person, more willing to fight for myself and to fight for what is right. Being underestimated is actually a position of power. Anyone who is thought of as less is assumed to be weak and complacent; that assumption creates an arrogance that is a giant blind spot. People have underestimated me, for sure, but most of the time it is the world that discounts me.

We live in a culture of "NO." It is in every part of our society. "NO" is our mother culture. The world tells us "NO," every day, all day. Mother culture tells us this so much that we start to tell each other, "NO", too. And most of the time we also tell ourselves, "NO."

You cannot do that.
You cannot take that risk.
You cannot wear that.
You cannot speak up.
You cannot fail or make a fool of yourself.
You cannot ask for what you are worth.
You cannot... [Fill in the blank], FOREVER.

When I teach improvisational comedy, the first thing I must do is break down the culture of "NO," that hinders a performer's success. In an art form that depends on saying "YES", the culture of "NO" becomes visible on stage immediately. We are so good at telling others and ourselves "NO" that we don't even know it. Improv exposes this horrible truth and just happens to be something that I love. This truth is something I have always known since childhood, not solely for being a victim of the culture of "NO", but because, for most of my life, I have just lived in the "YES" mode.

Why? How, you ask? I do not know. I don't know why I have always believed in myself. Why don't I accept disappointment? Why I am always positive and why do I never wallow in defeat? Why I don't accept being in a funk or depression? I am human and have suffered disappointments and

e never let them define me. If you don't fail, then you've
good. Michael Jordan was cut from the varsity team.
rdan, the greatest basketball player of all time!

.........ly had moments where I didn't like my body, but quickly recognized this as the world telling me "NO". I decided to have a lifelong policy to love my body. My body is doing everything right. I celebrate every year I get older. I celebrate every gray hair. I celebrate my body, period. I will not let the world tell me I am wrong, and I am DAMN sure am not letting the world (or any piece-of-shit human) make me feel bad about my body. The older I get, the cooler I get; that goes for all of us. Anytime we let mother culture's "NO" into our minds, it creates a groove in our brain. The groove becomes deeper each time we use it. These paths can be very difficult to break down. It takes zero effort to give into this. It takes no effort to default to the negative and create a million trails of self-doubt in our brains. But: anyone can break down those paths and forge new ones. This is what I believe is most daunting and difficult for people.

I made my own stilts as a child and taught myself how to walk on them. There were a few prototypes of failed versions. One time a foot support came loose, and on the way down I cut my leg on three exposed nails. I lost balance hundreds of times. But making the stilts and learning how to walk on stilts never seemed impossible. No one was literally saying "NO" to me, but the expressions on my friends' faces did. This was a big moment in noticing the difference between me and others when it came to the culture of "NO." Making anything, let alone stilts, was unfeasible to my peers. To me, it was merely a decision of whether to do the work or not. Stilts could have been straight A's, another language, a sport, or anything I wanted. I was not limiting myself where my friends had already started.

When I was 18, I did not go off to a big-box college, but instead, I decided that I stay home, go to community college, and saved every penny to travel Europe for the following summer. Did I ever experience the world telling me "NO!" Every person I told about my plans to go to Europe told me not to go, or were insultingly baffled by my decision. There is a huge American chunk of the culture, telling Americans not to leave their country.

They don't like us.
You will get robbed.
It is too scary.
It is too difficult.

It is all nonsense. The American culture of "NO" can suck my dick. I was not hearing any of it; I went to Europe at the height of the George W. Bush presidency with zero problems. In fact, I had a completely fantastic, educational, enlightening, and transformative experience. What if I had listened to all of those "NOs?" How many "NOs" have I listened to unknowingly? How many had I let into my life to create a Pacific Crest Trail in my brain? That possibility of listening to mother culture was what was scary to me. I started listening to mother culture about other things of substance: things that were actually important

I used to think that I could not be gay because I could not let everyone who was mean to me be right. I could not let them win. All the people at my church in my small town looked at me like I was a fucking freak. I could not let them win. I could not let my teachers who shamed me for using my hands too much when I talked win. I could not let all the people who told me I acting like a girl win. I could not let my Uncle calling me faggy at the family card table win.

This was listening to mother culture in the worst way. I always knew I was gay, ever since I can remember, and I never felt there was something wrong with me. In fact, when being told homosexuality is wrong by my church, I remember thinking even as a very small child, "But wait, I am gay and nothing is abnormal with me, so this must be bullshit." (This was the beginning of my journey to becoming an agnostic). How did I lose this knowledge? How could I let the world tell me who I was and that I was wrong? Especially after just bragging at the beginning of this introduction about how ahead of the game I was ad nauseam. How could I let the world convince me I was straight? That is how powerful the culture of "NO," is. If you listen to it, mother culture will not allow you to walk on stilts, travel Europe, or be yourself.

Awareness is the first step. Recognize that the world will never stop telling you "NO." Understand you will be underestimated every day you walk this earth. The second step is to defy "NO." Rebuke it. Stop listening to mother culture; stop running the paths she and YOU have created in your brain. Know that it will be easier the more you fight. Find power in being underestimated. Be yourself and WIN.

"Life is what you make it."

Words are the wind for sure, but the intention is REAL. If you want to have a full and enriching life, then you have to make it happen. No one is going to do it for you. No one cares enough about you to do that. If you reject the culture of negativity and forge a positive outlook and optimism on all things in your life, then your life is going to kick ASS!

VOLUNTEER VICTIM

Advice: If you are going to get into a mass plane crash, do not do it in Anchorage, Alaska; the fire fighters are not prepared to save your life.

For many years I had to be CPR/First Aid-certified for my job. I took the class every year. There is always a part where the instructor partners up the whole class and one person is the victim and the other is the rescuer. There is only enough time in the class to do the exercise once, so most of the time the partnership will not switch from victim to rescuer and vice versa. Because I take the class every year, I know this is coming and anticipate it. I do this because one of my favorite things to do is pretend to be a victim with a stranger who is trying to do CPR, flip my body over, or drag me correctly out of a "burning building". I commit to being 100% dead weight. Most people who play the CPR victim will help out; they'll kind of flip themselves over rather than having a stranger really touch them. I LOVE it and secretly enjoy my front row seat to their surprise at me not helping them as they struggle to move my 250-pound body.

I got to experience this enjoyment to its fullest when I visited my friend in Alaska. We were talking over the phone about my upcoming visit and she said, "Oh, by the way, I went ahead and signed us up to volunteer to pretend to be victims in a mass plane crash simulation at Ted Stevens International Airport. Are you down?"

I replied, "This is why we are friends. Thank you." I am so ready to be on Oceanic flight 815[1]. Then before I know it I'm in Alaska and we're at the airport, and right from the start, it is a dream come true. When we arrive, we are giving badges with what our role is. Some people were the walking wounded; some were dead; some were unconscious. I had the pleasure of being assigned a broken left tarsal. They also instructed us that we were not to speak or respond to English. They wanted to simulate a plane crash from another country's airline, one where the victims would not speak or understand the language of the rescuers.

To make sure we understood the rules, the trainers quickly yell "LOOK OVER THERE!" while pointing to his left. All of us volunteers look. The trainer says, "You have all failed. When we do the simulation as best you can pretend to not understand English. Act the part and take it seriously." This is all to better train emergency responders of the city of Anchorage. It

---

1 Who was into *Lost*? I was lost in the *Lost*. So many unanswered questions, and all I wanted was more, give me more questions! I want to be *Lost*!

is also music to my ears. They are preaching to the choir and do not need to tell me twice.

We head out and get into position, which is on the tarmac in between active runways. Planes are landing and taking off all around us, and God only knows what the people on those planes think is happening. There are lifeless looking bodies on the ground, aimless survivors walking around, and a big old piece of the airplane is partially on fire. Instead of a plane, they had two city buses on the tarmac to represent the crashed plane. In Anchorage, they call city buses People Movers, which somehow seems demeaning with a sprinkle of racism to me. I was assigned to be a victim on the People Mover, but I thought my talents would be better suited outside the plane amongst the walking wounded, the dead, and the real lost and found luggage of the Ted Stevens International Airport. I made this decision because, after all, I am a trained method actor and I also discovered that the victims still on the plane are the last to be rescued[2].

They blow the whistle and someone yells, "Start acting. The simulation is beginning!" All but a handful of volunteers are not acting like they were actually in a plane crash. Their lack of enthusiasm really pisses me off, but it does not stop the Jay Train. I am committed to portraying a realistic broken left ankle.

Before any of the rescue workers could get to the scene, they had to put out the fake fire for a full ten minutes. Halfway through, they all just turned around and left. Apparently, there is a real emergency in Anchorage and they have to go save the day somewhere else. An hour later, they blow the whistle and say, "They are coming back, start acting." Game on.

After putting out the fake fire again, it is the firefighters who come on the scene to save the people, while the police stay in the safe zone helping victims and getting IDs. The cops are really into this exercise and taking it seriously. The firefighters are not. They slump onto the scene and break character and the fourth wall. They are mean to the volunteers, they make fun of us, and in general are being jerks (the way most firefighters actually are).[3] The Firefighters are not really participating. You can tell that they are

---

[2] Plane Crash Survival Tip: Do not let yourself be left on the plane when it crashes because rescuers will put out the fire first, save all the people outside the plane, THEN get to you. At which point you will be dead.

[3] I really like how in Alaska, the hero is not the firefighter. It is the Bush Pilot. The Bush Pilot is what kids who grow up in Alaska want to be. There are no roads in

only doing this because they had to, and are pouting their way through it. Volunteer Victims are commanded to stop acting by the firefighters. Near me is one guy who is supposed to be unconscious and in a coma and needs to be taken via a gurney to the safe zone. The firefighters bring the gurney over and tell him that this is only a simulation and they are not going to pick him up. Out of the corner of his conflicted mouth, he says, "But I am in a coma…" They bark a harshly back at him to walk back himself.

The other volunteers are breaking left and right, succumbing to these bullish tactics. But not me. I have a broken left tarsal and they are going to save me. I scream in gibberish like a champion, don't they know I can speak in tongues? I do not give in. By God, I have a broken left tarsal and they are going to get me to the safe zone.

It takes two full grown firefighters to pick my ass up and carry me to the safety zone. I scream in pain the whole way. They mock me the entire time, asking if I am going to milk this all the way to the end. Luckily none of those words hurt my feelings because I didn't speak English. In my mind I am Korean and I speak only Korean. I was Jin-Soo Kwon from Lost. Their words slip off of me like water off a Korean duck's back.

In closing: the firefighters lived up to every negative stereotype and prejudice I harbor against them. They are not heroes, and NO, I didn't forget about 9/11. This volunteer victim won! Please assume that I will get up on my own volition and walk on this broken left tarsal. Please assume that because you got C's in high school, I will respect you and be intimidated by your presentation of masculinity. Please do all of that, because it will not work. Long live the volunteer victims!

[Insert Crowd Applauding]

Alaska, you have to fly everywhere. Especially in the villages. You have to fly and Bush Pilots are bad asses! Nobody cares about firefighters, and that is how it should be. Let's face it. Most firefighters are dicks. It is like your whole high school baseball team grew up to be fire fighters and baseball players are the scum of the earth. I have seen a group of firefighters hit a ball out of a kid's hand on a playground and high five his buddies, like it was out of movie. They are not heroes. They are bullies.

METH JOGGER

I used to be a bicyclist. I exclusively biked for eight years. Then I got a car. Right around the same time, I was diagnosed with car-fat. Car-fat can happen to anyone. When I got diagnosed with car-fat, I decided to do something about it and started jogging.

I have been jogging now for 3 years. Hold the applause; I am not a hero. The heroes are the firefighters. (Just kidding, they're a bunch of dicks.) I am now up to running six miles without stopping. I jog in my neighborhood because my neighborhood is my gym. And I jog at night because there is a shit ton of people at my gym in the daytime. I also don't like people looking and staring at my car-fat. Therefore, I jog at night in my neighborhood and I do the same loop every time. My neighborhood buttons up to a freeway. For a portion of my sidewalk jog, to my right is on-coming freeway traffic and neighborhood to my left. In between the sidewalk and the neighborhood is a sizable rhododendron hedge. Concealed in that rhododendron hedge from the eyes of society is a healthy meth village.

I don't have any problems with the meth village inhabitance. Mostly out of sight, out of mind. I have heard all the telltale sounds: angry yelling, scratching, pit bulls on rope leashes, and cats being forced to live on human shoulders.

The quiet peace of my run was disrupted one evening around dusk, which is lighter out than I would prefer because of my car-fat. On a straight away along the freeway stretch, my attention was grabbed by an erratic meth head with a skullet. He was in a loop of looking back and then dead sprinting left and right. Suddenly stopping, playing it cool, walking as if no one can tell he was high. Looking back and then dead sprinting as if he was running for his life.

I realized that when looking back, he is looking at me... and believes I am chasing him. Game on. (Torturing people on drugs: I get it from my mother.)

Every time he looked back, I made myself bigger and more foreboding. One time I threateningly pointed right at him and yelled "YOU!" when he looked back. He swerved into traffic and nearly collided with a car. This was all fun and games until I got close to him (which I should have put together myself since I was running towards this hot mess).

Once I got close, the meth head realized I was just a muggle, just a citizen trying to get some exercise. Right as I pass him he gargled out something indiscernible. There was no way in hell I was sticking around for the toothless wonder and I kept jogging. The meth head wanted to say something so bad to me that he started to chase ME!

Me chasing him that was a joke. He chasing me was not a joke. It was very real and I don't know if you know this but meth heads can run very fast. Luckily, I can run faster when motivated by meth death.

BAD TIPPER

I am a bad tipper. It is a character flaw that I am okay with. When people discover this fact about me, they are aghast; it is a cardinal American sin. I have always felt European and/or Japanese about what we call gratuity. Getting tips is cool but I like to tip on my terms and in situations where I want to give someone a tip. I love to give the person pumping my gas a dollar tip because it blows their mind that I would tip them. It surprises them because our culture says we don't tip gas pumpers, but we tip taxi drivers. This is why I love Lyft. It is just assumed that you have to tip a taxi driver who sucks. Society hits us over the head with the law in which we must tip waiters in restaurants or we are bad people.

A friend of mine told me the best gift he ever got was a tip calculator card so he would know what to tip. Disgusting! Fifteen percent? Twenty percent? How about tipping what you feel is right? The way I see it, part of the problem is assessing how much work I am actually costing this server. When it is counter service/bus your own, you can fucking forget about getting a tip from me. At that point, I am pitching in on your job duties. The last real job I had was a split shift and I would have to work very early in the morning Monday through Friday. I would also get off work very early, like eight fucking AM. I made it a habit of dropping in at a breakfast joint in my neighborhood once or twice a week, around 8:30 AM.

There were two servers on the morning shift in the week; it was one or the other. One was my friend. She was a really warm person who was a joy to be served by. I enjoyed tipping her a fair amount. The other server was not warm and we didn't enjoy each other. She was a run-down 34-going-on-43-year-old, and too old to still be a goth. I could never figure out the schedule for which server was going to be there. The last time I ever went into that restaurant, I came up short on the goth breakfast roulette and drew Alice Cooper. For some reason, the restaurant was uncharacteristically full of people, and Sid Vicious sat me across the full room of breakfast goers. I ordered the same damn thing I always order[4], this order including my coffee with honey and cream. She begrudgingly brought my coffee and slopped down the honey, twerking around to sulk elsewhere. I immediately noticed the jar of honey was covered with sugar ants. Just crawling with them.

With one finger, I pushed the jar of honey to the very edge of my table.

---

[4] If you find yourself at Genies Café, order: Biscuits n' Gravy, O'Brien potatoes, two eggs over easy, and a side of bacon.

Across the parted waters of little piggies stuffing their faces, the Ramsey to my Moses looked over, saw what I had done, and shot me with a nonverbal gesture which screamed, "WHAT!?! What's wrong with you?"

Not wanting to yell across a crowded restaurant, I non-verbally motioned for her to come back to my table. She doesn't move those ill-fitting hot topic jeans an inch and now verbally shouted across the crowded diner, "What's wrong with the honey?"

I told her to, "Come here" and motion a non-threatening finger to my lips accompanied by a playful, "Shhhh." At this point, many piggies started to follow this exchange.

Billy Corgan reluctantly slopped across the Sea of Galilee right up to my table and said, "What's wrong?"

"Um… there are ants on that honey," repeating my non-threatening finger to my lips and, "Shhhh."

"There are ants on the honey? What? Where?" The Cthulhu blurted out.

In a hushed tone, I said: "Right there," and pointed to the sides of the honey and the few ants crawling on the table.

"Oh…." Comprehension was finally visible on the stunted face of Ozzy Osbourne.

Then a horrifically tacky action was taken. SQUISH. SQUISH. SQUISH. She ended the life of three ants on the table right in front of me, on the table I am about to eat on. She wiped off the honey with a beaten up kitchen rag and called it good.

Monetarily, I could not offer any tip as a self-respecting person. But the situational and the teachable moments I thought were of a high value and self-evident:

1. Do not knowingly or unknowingly serve anyone food items crawling with ants.

2. Do not bate a customer in yelling across a packed restaurant of eating people that you just served them something covered in ants.

3. If you find yourself skipping teachable moments 1 & 2, offer the customer any combination of these options: an apology, moving tables, or a complimentary meal. Do NOT execute ants on the table and leave the corpses as a garnish.

"If you don't fail, then you've failed."

The fear of doing something wrong, or silly, or
looking stupid is crippling. Let yourself fail.
In failure, we learn, celebrate, and play.
The world tells adults to stop playing... why?
Why should we stop playing?
That sounds horrible.

AMBULANCES

My family didn't go on big vacations; instead, we went camping every year. My parents had bought a trailer-camper and had a Fierce Ford Aerostar to pull it anywhere in the Pacific Northwest. Often times we would camp near the coast, go crabbing for the day and come back to eat crab and butter all night. We did go horse camping one summer due to my mother's stint as a horse person.

[Divergence:]
Of all the different types of animal people, horse people are the weirdest. My mother (and, vicariously, my sister and I) found out real quick, thank God. The fascination came from my mother renting our unused pasture to horse owners. I met so many freaks coming to my house from the sticks to care for their horse. One whackjob horse lady traded pasture rental for riding lessons for my mother, sister, and myself[5].

During that particular summer in the middle of my families horse dynasty, we were invited to go horse camping with whackjob's friends. Driving to the campground, whackjob asked if I could co-pilot the drive with her in her beefy truck. It was… alright. Once we got there, we met whackjob's friends: a sprawling, white trash, multi-family…but who isn't in the horse community? There were younguns in the mix, but none that were my or my sister's age. They did have several scary-ass Rottweilers in addition to the horses. These dogs were big, scary, and all of their commands were in German. Years later, as an adult, I brought up that odd camping trip with my parents and they said, "Oh yeah, now that you are older, all of those people were white supremacists. We didn't know that going in and we are sorry."

Were my parents on to something? Are all horse people racist? I'll let you decide.

[Back on Track:]

The only real family vacation the Flewelling's took in my childhood was an ambulance road trip. My father was a paramedic who climbed the corporate ladder all the way to being a vice president of an ambulance company, in charge of Washington, Oregon, and California, all without a college education. When he was the boss, every paramedic I ran into in the world, I

---

[5] Yes, I can ride a horse if need be.

would ask them, "Do you know Keith Flewelling?"
"Yes."
"He is my Dad."
"Oh…cool."
"My dad can fire you."

I thought it was funny; I still do. My father had to yell at me to get me to stop, "It is not funny to tell paramedics that I can fire them. It is not FUNNY!" I did stop, but I still think it is kind of funny.

Back in the 1990s, my father's company would offer employees $3,000 to pick up the brand new ambulance from the factoring in Tennessee and drive it back to Portland, Oregon. My family did it twice before it became more cost-effective to ship the ambulances by train. Each time, my parents would get two ambulances and drive both of them at the same time in tandem. The first trip we drove back along the south and up California; the second trip we took the Northern route back.

This was kid heaven… at least for me it was. My sister and I are very different people and a very telling fact about these trips illustrate the difference more than anything. The entirety of each trip I spent in the back of a brand new, fully equipped ambulance, while my sister spent every mile sitting in the front seat like an adult. I have so many fond memories of being in those ambulances. My parents would not let me turn on the emergency lights, but they would let me get on the outside microphone. An endless field of cows were victims to my childhood voice yelling noises and all the hits from Aladdin. Kid heaven.

There are so many benefits to taking an ambulance on a road trip. Mainly, everyone on the road moved out of our way. It was magic. People gave way to us and gave up choice parking spots the whole trip. Adult heaven.

Unfortunately, you can also get into disappointing situations, like the one we experienced in Arizona. Going to the Grand Canyon, we made our way through very windy roads. We whipped around the corner and came upon a fresh car crash. It had just happened. Passing cars just stopped moments ago. One car was on its roof. There was a dazed man on the side of the road with blood covering his face sitting up next to an unconscious man not moving. I remember making eye contact with the bloodied-face man. The lead good Samaritan (who was probably a fanny-pack dad) looked up from directing people in the rescue effort (because he took a CPR class once) to see two shiny new ambulances roll up to his crash scene. Fanny-pack Dad and all the supporting good Samaritans looked up as well. There

was a wave of facial expressions that occurred in slow motion.
Yes!
The paramedics are here!
Wow, they got here so fast. How did they do that? Oh well.

The bloodied-faced man's face expressed all of these sentiments as if to say, "*I am all right. And now that the paramedics are here, my unconscious friend will be alright too.*" Then as he made eye contact with me, a child sitting out-of-place in an ambulance. His face changed to confusion and foreboding as if to say, "*Sorry, friend. You are not going to make it.*"

Fanny-pack Dad ran in front of us, waving his hands like a pro, just in case we accidentally missed the crash and kept driving. When my family jumped out of the vehicles was when Fanny-pack Dad and good Samaritans' expressions caught up to Bloodied-faced Man.

Where are the paramedics?
Whose kids are those?
What kind of sick joke is this?

Fanny Pack Dad could not compute this situation and was pissed. He shifted into 'dad mode' to investigation and grilled my dad. The bleeding victims were the second priority now that he needed to get to the bottom of this situation. He could not process what my dad told him. It almost got through his pleated khakis when my dad told him that he was technically a paramedic, but was not licensed in the state and could not help. His dad brain imploded. The faces of the good Samaritan extras in the background melted with confusion mixed with scorn as we drove away.

Twenty minutes later, we had a hard time enjoying the Grand Canyon.

SMOKERS ARE SO SELFISH

We all have friends who have gone hipster on us. It is important to remember it is not our fault. It can happen to best of us. The worst is when you have a friend who is dating a hipster. When this happens, you really just have to grin and bear it. Of course you "like" the person your friend is dating and you just can't tell your friend that they are dating the biggest hipster idiot in Portland. And you really can't tell them that every pretentious thing they say makes you want to poop blood. Contradicting them in conversation, telling them they are too skinny, pointing out how stupid their glasses are, or that they are wearing too many necklaces is just not an option because the loyalty you have for your friend prevents you. Right?

One of my oldest friends starting dating this hipster named James. James fancied himself the height of fashion, an expert in "cool" music, and the smartest person in any room. Worse, my friend ended up dating James for a painfully long time. We shared good moments in our tethered-together friendship. But for the most part, our relationship, for me, was filled with hidden anger born from somehow always losing at every backgammon game to him and having to suffer through his incessant arrogant and foolhardy statements... A true hipster is always saying the stupidest shit with the air of superiority, because they're so smart that there is no way that they could possibly be wrong.

An example:

Pit bulls and attack dogs once came up in conversation. There was a general feeling that pit bulls are scary and we all agreed we never wished to be attacked by them (or really by any dog).

James barged into the conversation, claiming, "If a dog attacked me, I would just break its leg or punch it down its throat."

Duh, right? That was what we all would do if we were as smart as James. There was nothing I wanted more than for a Rottweiler to bust into that apartment and viciously attack just him. While everyone would be freaking out, all I would say while watching this incredible dream come true would be, "Break its leg! Why aren't you punching it down the throat? Why are you bleeding?"

I would have given anything for that to have happened right then. Unfortunately, it did not.

In the course of our trio friendship, we traveled Europe together. When you are hanging out or traveling with a couple it is always two against one, hipster or not. All group decisions were solved with this tyranny-of-the-couple philosophy: what we did, where we ate, and where we stayed had little to no input from me.

"Let's go check out Pere Lachaise Cemetery!"

"Well, we want to go shopping."

In order to save money in Paris, the three of us stayed in a single room on the 6th floor of a shady hotel and split it equally three ways. My equal share included sneaking in and out of the hotel every time we came and went because there were only "two" people staying in the room. Our room had just enough floor space for a double bed, so I slept on the floor without a pillow, and my backpack. The only redeeming quality was a petite balcony overlooking the rooftops of Paris. At the time, I was an avid cigarette smoker and found French cigarettes delicious. Smoking on the balcony was my only morsel of comfort in that French hotel. Our whole trip was played to this tune of Jay getting the shaft because the couple selfishly could out number me on all decisions.

Late one afternoon, in order to save money we bought food at a grocery store, to eat at the hotel and then we were to go out for drinks afterward. My dinner choice was a baguette with a hunk of an unknown French cheese. I had been warned before the trip about France's different regulations with regard to food safety, and that I might want to go with a more generic and safer cheese. But I was not to be deterred from my mystery cheese and, to the disgust of my vegan hipster compatriots, I went back to the hotel to eat the entire baguette and hunk of cheese all in one sitting.

Afterward, when they were ready to go out, I started to feel unwell. I decided to stay in for the night while they went out for drinks. Shortly after they left, my condition worsened, which resulted in me crawling out to the petite balcony to throw up all the freshly chewed bread and cheese. Feeling too weak to properly clean up my wet loaf creation I had just deposited on the narrow floor of the petite balcony, I merely crawled back to my corner of the floor, grabbed a pillow off the skanked-out bed, and promptly went to sleep. Later, the loud, drunken stumbling of the couple returning late interrupted my slumber, but I did not stir or indicate that I was awake. I heard inebriated hipster James kick off his pointed leather ankle boots and head out to the balcony. Seconds later I heard, "Oh, SICK!" My unintentional trap could not have been set more perfectly. Drunk James had stepped directly into my wet loaf of barely digested cheesy French baguette.

In the morning I woke up completely healed, refreshed, and wanting my much-awaited French morning cigarette. Upon surveying the scene I discovered a discarded barf-soaked white sock, and several left footprints leading back inside from the petite balcony. Right before I opened the balcony doors, the head of a haggard, viciously hung over hipster with a kinked neck minutely rose up from the shared pillow on the bed and said, "Don't open that door."

"I have to smoke," I said and opened the door.

The Parisian morning summer sun had thoroughly cooked up my French-American surprise, and the invigorating aroma rushed into the room like a rhinoceros charging at full speed. I watched the stench hit hipster James square in the face and knock his kinked neck back down on the shared pillow. Shortly after I lit my French cigarette, the summer vomit smell was followed by my second-hand smoke. This only compounded the suffering of the hungover sleeping couple. On the balcony was my dinner, I remember thinking that I really should quit smoking... but not today. Returning to the room and feeling even better after finishing my cigarette, I was met with a defeated comment from a motionless James.

"Smokers are so selfish." Just as selfish as couples, I thought.

ITALIAN DINNER

While traveling with my friend, José in Europe another time, we met our friends, Megan and James, in Switzerland. Megan was our friend and James was her boyfriend; that was important to note, a distinction I held. In Switzerland, we met a wonderful Australian named Marta, who was living in the United Kingdom and was on holiday as well. There were two hostels in Interlaken, Switzerland: one for drinkers and one for smokers. We all met at the hostel for the smokers, which was built out of an old farm. All of the hedges on the grounds (which were well over my head) were marijuana bushes, let grown wild. The five of us hit it off and had a jolly ol' time in Switzerland and agreed to meet up in Italy in a week's time.

We didn't meet in just anywhere in Italy; we met in Cinque Terre, which is a string of five tiny villages on the Mediterranean coast. It was heaven. Any Italian cooking book in the world has a picture of the Cinque Terre on the cover, it is that beautiful. We stayed in the most southern village, which was the least touristy. All of the villages were connected by a hiking trail and a rickety, old Italian train, where everyone smoked despite No Smoking signs being visible everywhere[6] . One day, we paid the one Euro to ride the smoky train up to the northern most village and hiked back. This was picturesque. Everything was beautiful and had an old world feel of simplicity. The village we stayed in was surrounded by fragrant lemon orchards which would mix up with the night's breeze and salt from the ocean to create the most invigorating summer nights.

Five of us started this adventure, but Marta met two Californians on the way and brought them with her. Now seven strong, we rented a top floor apartment with a rooftop view of the village and ocean below for pennies once it was split seven ways. The same method was used to feed ourselves as well. Jose and I had paid for nights in Rome that we decided to eat the money because we were having too much fun in by ocean with friends new and old.

Our days in Cinque Terre looked like this:

- We woke up around 11:00 AM.

- Everyone would throw in 2 Euros for enough margarita pizza to feed Haiti.

- Then we would lazily make our way down to the ocean to crawl

[6] All of Europe is an ashtray.

through Italians and Swedes for space on the rocky cliffs to lie in the sun and swim in the Mediterranean ocean.

- After a swim and a nap, we would all throw in five euros for groceries to make our own dinners.

- Post-feast, we would make our way down to the family-owned bar and drink chilled limoncello made from the lemon orchards surrounding us.

- We would dance and drink and laugh the night away. Pure heaven.

On an afternoon swim, my dearest friend, Megan, and I swam a great distance to bask and rest on another rocky cliff with the village in view. We ended up diving into deep conversations about our friendship and ambitions. We dreamed together of making it big and made a pact to help each other and bring each other along with our success. That conversation meant the world to me and the long swim back only made it that much more important[7].

The two Californians were everything you imagine they would be: blonde, surfers, and dim. All true Californian traits. Apart of our ragtag crew for sure, but they were having their own friendship saga. We all at great length were told of their friendship growing up together and this trip together was the last hurrah for them. One of them was a natural James Dean character. It was effortless for him to walk around shirtless and attractive, a carefree rebel-without-a-cause demeanor. He was not bright but he didn't have to be because he was so cool and laid-back. He was sex walking.

His friend was definitely the sidekick character. He was on the same level as James Dean in being shirtless and attractive, but horribly lacking in any bit of coolness. He reeked of desperation for James Dean's approval. This trip was huge for him and clearly his planning. I would not have been surprised if he had paid for some portion for James Dean, who probably could have taken or left it. But his childhood friend paying for it won him over.

We met the Californians when Marta rolled in a day after the Oregonians. Being nice fellows and a friend of Marta's, we were happy to take their money and offer them the floor to sleep on. We were quickly informed by the sidekick[8] the pair had just got matching pukka shell, "best friend"

---

[7] Megan and I are still friends and still help and enjoy each other.
[8] Californians are all chatty Cathy's—and don't think for one moment that they are actually listening to anything you have to say.

necklaces, which even by 2003 standards were outdated. Wearing that necklace was a dream come true for the sidekick; for James Dean, it was worn with nonchalance.

One evening the sidekick missed dinner and came into the apartment looking defeated, not wearing his prized necklace which represented the love of his cool best friend and the level of coolness he would never achieve. While swimming in the ocean earlier in the day, he lost his cherished necklace. After he became aware of its disappearance, he had spent the dinner hours in a desperate furry with a cheap snorkel and goggles, thoroughly searching the ocean for it. Somehow it eluded him, and he was crushed. Even more crushing was the fact that James Dean had not joined in the search; he had eaten dinner (which was delicious), and discarded his own necklace shortly after.

[Stage Direction]

[Sidekick, physically exhausted, eyes red from the salt water, clearly sad, looks up to James Dean and notices he was not wearing his half of the matching best friend pukka shell necklaces.]

Sidekick: "You are not wearing your necklace."

James Dean: "…Yeah, it is in my bag."

Sidekick: "I am going to look again tomorrow; I only stopped looking because the sun went down."

James Dean: "I just figured that since you don't have yours, I won't wear mine."

Sidekick: "You can still wear it even though I don't have mine." James Dean: [With a stern look and the tone of finality] "You need to let this go, man."

[Sidekick tears up a bit while pretending he was not. Sidekick excited rooftop dinner table set with a vague mention of needing to go to the bathroom. Livingroom cast continued laughing and drinking wine for the rest of the night.]

[End Scene]

On the last night in our Italian apartment, the seven of us (who had created and shared such a beautiful experience) decided to have a feast. Chipping in a bit more, we could make a banquet that would make the Dominican

Republic jealous. What most Americans don't understand is that the food in Italy is better than anything we have in the states. Anything you buy, even if it is packaged or in a can, is made from the best stuff on earth. It is indescribably better food. With Megan at the helm, we made a gorgeous meal. My contribution was a lackluster mac and cheese (but we don't need to dwell on that aspect of this story). Everyone gave their money at lunch and went their separate ways knowing dinner was at 8:00 PM. After our afternoon swim, no Californians came home. Preparing the meal, still no Californians. Setting the table with candles, no Californians. We forged ahead with one of the best meals of our lives, surrounded by close friends and the setting sun on the Mediterranean Ocean.

With our bellies full and basking in the aftermath of the feast, in stumbled the two Californians, head to bloody toe in what appeared to be dust from a coal mine. They had the look of surviving a near-death experience.

Having not done the hike between the five villages yet, the Californians had headed out after lunch in the direction of the most northern village. They then decided to forego paying roughly one American dollar for a train ticket, and instead ride like a cheap-ass Californian. Seeing how these train tickets were important, the conductor promptly caught them. Instead of feigning ignorance and trying to pay for a ticket, or even accepting the twenty-Euro fine, they decided as the train pulled into the next village to dash off the train with the conductor in pursuit. Now instead of running through the village and getting back on the hiking trail, they decided to hide and let the train leave the station, and then walk along the train tracks back. These are, mind you, train tracks that go through several tunnels and, for the most part, terrifyingly close to deathly high cliffs. (Hey, they were on a best friend adventure alright? Hang ten, brah.)

Upon entering the tunnels, they quickly discovered they were pitch black. (Who knew?) Since they could not see, they felt along the sides of the walls and held hands; Sidekick loved this so hard. Their tan Californian fingers rubbing the walls disturbed the dry blackish dust pollution that made up the walls of the tunnel and swiftly attached itself thickly to their shirtless and fearful bodies. The blackish dust also loved the eyes and set up shop in there as well. It warrants a mention that flip flops were the wrong choice for an adventure walking/running in the dark, on uneven ground, and an environment not designed for humans to walk on. If I was a betting man, I would have lost money on those bloody toes.

Halfway home, in the middle of a long dark tunnel the two Californians heard the sound of a distant and approaching train. It was in this moment they remembered the train ran every half an hour. They doubly realized there was only enough space in this tunnel for one rickety Italian train that was fast approaching. The slow, hand-holding, wall-molesting walk turned into a frantic dead sprint for their lives! They were not going to make it out of the tunnel in time. Death was upon them (Sidekick would've probably been okay with going out with his bro like this). But just in the nick of time, they came upon a doorway alcove indent into the wall. They jammed their bodies into the tiny nook as the rickety train stormed by. Due to the close quarters, their junk probably touched and Sidekick loved it so hard again.

Astonished, the dinner party politely held back obvious observations about the situation, cruel truths, and countless alternative choices that could have been made. But instead, we offered them cold leftovers. They absently ate in a PTSD silence as the dinner party carried on in our merriment.

SMELLI CARELLI

I met Smelli Carelli working indirectly together for a nonprofit in Portland. She was from Albany but lived in Portland to go to Reed College. Once on a bus trip, she told me about a program in which she had done the previous summer, where you're sent out to villages in Alaska to run day camps for kids. Because of this experience, Smelli developed what she called a "passion" for anything Alaskan, in particular, anything concerning the Native Alaskans: the history and way of life. This "passion" resulted in a very annoying self-belief she was an expert on the subject, despite the fact that she was a gangly, redheaded, white girl from New York. Soon following that conversation, I applied for a position with the program, was hired, and coincidently partnered with Smelli Carelli. This was how I got to know Smelli Carelli intimately.

Reed College is a pretentious school, which attracts similarly pretentious students, some hiding it better than others. Most Reed students are very smart; they work very hard, but they also play very hard, with drugs. We all know people in our lives who are extremely intelligent but just happen to be drug enthusiasts. What can you do? You can always pick out a 'Reedie' by the telltale sign of them not shutting the fuck up about it. It is as if the conversation was driven by the need to mention Reed College at every turn. Reed hosts Renn Fayre, the largest private party in the state of Oregon, every June. This weekend-long party is to open to all current students and alumni in order to congratulate the recent graduates, but the real reason is to toast to how smart they all believe themselves to be and do a lot of drugs. A couple years ago, they brought one of my favorite hip-hop artists to perform at Renn Fayre. It was rumored he agreed to come not for money, but for a thousand dollars' worth of coke. Sounds right.

Smelli Carelli went to Reed and was a philosophy graduate (if you can imagine that). I must admit, I have a personal distaste of philosophy majors. Philosophy is the most useless degree because it gives the user a false sense of superiority as if they are the only people who can read Beyond Good and Evil and not turn into a Nazi. Secondly, how many Karl Marxes do we need really? Beyond pondering existence, Smelli was into drugs. She boasted about having tried every drug except one. What was this lonely drug? The name I cannot remember, probably because it was invented by a chemistry major. Doing every drug is really nothing to brag about, especially when you do the math and realize that means you've done meth. But like most drug enthusiasts, there was more talking than doing.

Smelli had a quest to prove she was the smartest person where ever she went, and in the bush of Alaska, I was her only competition. An ongoing battle of wits ensued. Although I did not instigate the battle, I was more than happy to come out victorious. One tactic she used was to rattle off information on any subject, which most of it was irrelevant and only memorized in order to regurgitate later, to come out looking like she was intelligent. But her predominate strategy was to make me look like a fool in front of the kids by pointing out very obvious conclusions as if I were a confused foreigner. Example: We were following some kids through town and there was a fork in the road, one way sunny and the other shaded. One kid said, "Let's go this way. It's too hot to go that way." I repeated that phrase because it was cute and I am a repeater. Smelli turned to me and said, "That way is sunny; this way is shaded and it's cooler in the shade." Well, no shit. Another time she asked me when I was leaving whether I knew my way home, which was less than 2 blocks away. Fuck you.

I didn't have to do much to win the battle, due to the fact Smelli was and is a HUGE SLOB. She was the second sloppiest person I have ever encountered in my life. Naturally, my many victories over Smelli Carelli were actually done by herself. She lost everything, ate with her fingers, broke her camera, once a pair of her pants molded and she continued to wear them. She brought a fishing pole which never once touched the water. She brought a harmonica which never made a noise, despite her summer goal of learning how to play. A kid stole her harmonica once and she threw a bitch fit to get it back. And yet I still never heard her play that harmonica. After swimming she would walk barefoot up out of the water towards her shoes, collecting sand and pebbles on the bottom of her feet, then jam her sandy/rocky foot in a worn-out sock, then right into her consistently damp shoe. Her sloppiness reached new and exciting levels in the bush of Alaska.

Smelli was a horrible cook and ate with her fingers like an animal. When it came to boxed mac and cheese, a delicacy in the bush, she never completely stirred in the cheese powder. It would just be a bowl of yellow clusters of dried cheese powder strung about her blasé noodles. While watching her unknowingly choke down the pasta, I was mystified by someone who considered themselves so smart, but did not understand the remedy to this bowl of mac and cheese was to just keep stirring the powder in. Just a little bit more stirring, that's it.

Arlo was an awesome individual who befriended us. He was intelligent, friendly, and wanted to show us cool stuff in his village that he was rightly proud of. He decided to take us hunting in the morning. I did not want to get up that early but was convinced to go by Smelli, who kept going on and on about how this was a cultural experience. It would be rude to refuse, and if I didn't go, she couldn't. I agreed to go. We went hiking through the tundra in search of spruce hens. One presented itself, I missed once… twice… and on my third round, Arlo assisted me and I shot and killed it. The second spruce hen presented itself and it was Smelli's turn. She missed eight times in a row, even with Arlo standing behind her, looking down her sights and offering her direction. The spruce hen finally got a clue and flew away. Walking back, Arlo stopped and asked Smelli, jokingly to conceal seriousness, if she was actually trying to hit the bird. She played it off like she was a stupid girl and just couldn't get it. The next day while walking, she laughingly asked me if I noticed her purposely missing the bird yesterday.

"No."

"Yeah, I totally was missing on purpose."

"Why?"

"I didn't want to gut it and ya know."

"What about sustainability?"

"Well… I didn't need to eat the bird…"

"But you ate some of my bird."

"It was already dead and I didn't want to waste."

"Why didn't you just say no?"

"I didn't want to say no."

"He asked you if you missed on purpose and you lied to his face."

"Well… I just didn't want to gut the bird."

"Now you are just another white person to lie to a Native Alaskan."

She really didn't like it when I said that. And the rest of the summer didn't go so well.

I was in shock. For all the times she talked about the romantic way of subsistence living as the way of the native people of Alaska when it came down to it, it didn't mean a damn thing. The worst part was Arlo knew she was missing, after everything he had done for us. He had made us feel welcome, showed us cool stuff, took the day off work, and bullets are not cheap[9].

What I learned from that experience was about the character of Smelli Carelli. This character is a white woman who has an affinity towards a minority or disenfranchised group and, because of this affinity, they know everything about that minority/disenfranchised group: their plight, their struggles, and all the complex historical contexts and institutional discrimination against that group. You guys, they "get it". They've read one book. We have all met this character and will continue to meet this character in our lives. I now know how to spot them early and how to deal. Moreover, watching Smelli embarrass herself I learned when it comes to the experience of a minority or disenfranchised group, as white people, that is not a time for us to talk. That is a time for us to listen.

---

[9] Everything in the villages of Alaska is fucking expensive! A gallon of milk is like $15 and bullets are one the most expensive items; each round is $5-$8. So between Smelli and myself, we blew like $50 bucks of Arlo's money.

"The best gifts you ever receive in your life will be from yourself."

— Jay Flewelling

This phrase jumped out of my mouth when I was teaching school age students once. The reaction was firstly excited and then understanding turned the room to a sad gloom realization. It is true though.
What are your favorite things/items/tools/wardrobe pieces?
They all came from YOU.
Therefore, give yourself presents often.

LOVE. PROUD.

Guest Chapter by Marisa Latico

On the first experience, your face is most likely glued to the window of your small Cesena three-seater, drooling over the vast wilderness of rural Alaska. The expectations you might have had prior to embarking on this adventure are now shattered into a realm of unreal awe. It's something you can't explain; you just have to experience. Your thoughts of wanderlust and adventure are interrupted as the pilot shouts over the roar of the engine and points, "There, right there, is your home for the next two weeks."

Your initial thought is: "Where?" Then, just below the horizon, you see a scattering of buildings, connected by a series of boardwalks on dirt paths, and a larger strip of gravel, which you can only assume is the runway. As you grow closer, you see activity: four-wheelers speed toward the landing strip, bodies emerge from their dwellings searching the sky to see what has come to their tiny village, boats fish in the river, and the bustle of subsistent chores being accomplished by inhabitants in-between buildings.

You have arrived. As you step off the plane, start to unload, collect yourself, and try to wrap your brain around this new undertaking, you are greeted by the community and kids shouting, "Counselors!" They embrace you before you even have your bearings as if you are a long-lost relative returning home. Your new friends grab the abundant supplies that have traveled with you, welcoming you into their world, and embracing the world you bring to them.

You and your gear are shuttled to a large community hall via four-wheeler. Kids chase after, as you are paraded down the one road of the village. More and more people emerge and gather to see about the commotion. Shouts of "Counselors are here!" fill the air and you begin to understand the necessity of this unique camp program. You find an appreciation for the two weeks of training to understand Alaskan Native cultures and customs, the endless shopping for supplies, the hours of planning and packing as well as the time spent team building with your colleagues.

There is no rest for the weary. These kids have been awaiting this moment their entire summer. They come for the crafts, the games, camp outs, snacks, and swimming, but we all leave with so much more. You set up camp together, emptying boxes of glue, construction paper, paints, board games, cards, Modge Podge, brushes, Crayons, Frisbees, kickballs, tents, s'more supplies, and swimming gear. With each item and new box, their eyes grow with excitement… camp is in session!

The Rural Program of Alaska is not your ordinary camp program; it is so much more than you could ever imagine. It fulfills your sense of adventure. It builds your appreciation of connections. It allows you to be immersed in some of the most unique cultures, challenges you, and builds your sense of character and your appreciation for the little things. It was here, through this program that I met, befriended, and experienced a most difficult life event with Jay Flewelling.

Prior to the year I met Jay, as the director of the Rural Program, I worked as a counselor for six summers. It was a program that shaped a large majority of my college years and helped develop who I later became. This program has, and always will have, a special place in my heart. The experience, the friendships, and the independent growth that was created will never be lost on me and I will always be thankful for it. I think many of us who are alumni of this program would say the same. This program changes you for the better; it teaches you lessons you didn't even know you needed to learn. As I went into my first year as director, I was passionate about the mission, took this undertaking very seriously, and expected the same from the staff that I hired.

Jay was my fourth interview as the director. The interview process for our program, much like the program itself, was unique. We asked questions such as: "What would you do if you found a mouse in your camp? What would you do if an elder or youth came to your program drunk? How do you deal with conflict when you live, eat, sleep, and literally shit in the same area as your one and only co-worker?"

This program was mentally, physically, and emotionally taxing. In order to find the right candidate, we had to be candid as to what they might experience in these villages with limited communication and resources. Because the training for counselors was minimal, we relied on the candidates' ability to adjust and adapt independently. In a variety of situations, we provided two weeks of training prior to sending staff on six weeks of travel, two weeks in each village, with one or two other individuals, delivering meaningful, enriched, camp programs while maintaining respect for the community and culture that welcomed you.

After a phone interview with Jay, I was uncertain he was the right fit for the program. He had the experiences both with youth, wilderness, swimming, and just overall confidence in dealing with difficult situations. He was candid, had a great sense of humor, and seemed to bring an abundant amount of knowledge with games and activities in working with youth. However, he seemed to lack compassion and empathy for others and delicate situations. He was headstrong when it came to collaborating or compromising with others. Jay was black and white and I needed a gray area. Despite my reservations, I decided to offer him the job. His qualifications were just too great to pass up and I was confident that I could mold and shape some of the emotional and sensitivity he was lacking. Jay was first to arrive in Alaska, giving me an opportunity to get to know him better and strengthen our connection, building the ability to coach Jay for his journey into rural Alaska.

He was exactly what I expected: hardworking, task-driven and detail-oriented. He was my right-hand man for two days prior to all other staff arriving. We collected the majority of the supplies needed for that summer. I was able to delegate and trust him, establishing order to the chaos of the rural program. They were long days, but time seemed to fly while I was with him. We laughed and had an instant connection. The administrative piece of my new position was just frustrating. I was working in an office space that ran on specifics and the rural program was outside of anything you could plan. Jay understood the constraints of this work and supported me. Despite our instant professional connection, there was an emotional disconnect. He was there to give me a kick in the pants with work but, even to this day, I find myself wanting him to ask questions, listen, and be present with the emotional side of life. I continued to have my reservations, but he was successful with the Rural Program and in spite of my emotional needs, our friendship continued to blossom.

After that summer, we remained friends and grew close, traveling to visit each other, connecting, and always picking up where we left off. There was always a little piece missing for me, but it was one of those things that you accept. Friendships are give and take: a mixture of strengths and weaknesses, complements and compromises. I am an emotional being, more than most, and certainly more than Jay. Not that Jay is void of emotion, but often for me, it seemed when I brought up something dramatic or problematic, he would detach. It felt like there was a wall that kept him from engaging in this side our relationship. At times I walked away feeling a little uncertain of what he was really thinking or if I offended him or if he cared, but at the same time, I knew he was a friend.

The following summer, Jay came back to the program and we were to be paired together. I was excited, eager, happy, and a tad nervous to be working with my friend (he is a force to be reckoned with). We don't always see eye-to-eye. I feared for when we would disagree, how it would play out for not only our friendship but the entirety of the program. Either way, we were off. Following training, we drove to the airport to travel to our first village together. Passing by the sights I now call home, I received one of the most difficult phone calls of my life.

My mom's voice was shaking and I could tell she had been crying. She spoke softly to point it was difficult to hear her. I knew it was about my grandmother, who had been sick for some time. "Grams" was the most accepting woman. It is hard to put into the words the amount of support, love, knowledge, confidence, and sense of direction she bestowed on me. I attribute much of my emotional intelligence, compassion, and empathy to her. I try to honor her legacy every day. It was Grams, despite her sickness, who urged me to return to Alaska. She knew how much it meant to me and how it refreshed my soul. She got me. She was that one person who truly understood what I needed to thrive. Through it all, she was my rock.

My mom's words were numbing: Grams had been given three to five weeks to live. What was I to do? I was literally driving to the airport where I was fly to St. Mary's. Do I provide two weeks of the camp program, and then come back to spend time with her during her last days? Or do I not board a plane to St. Mary's but home to Buffalo? What would Grams do? Go. It was what we both wanted. I made up my mind and with a deep sigh, I asked my mom to put her on the phone. She had not spoken in days, but my intentions were to do all the talking and tell her the plan. I started, "Grams, it's Maris."

I paused, shaken by her labored breathing. I closed my eyes and was about to speak again when the rhythm of her breathing changed.

Then I heard a whisper, but was clearly her:

"Love. Proud."

Once again she offered everything I needed in that moment. (I carry those two words with me every day in a commemorative tattoo.) My intentions of the call were shattered as both I and the hospice room erupted in emotions. I gathered myself and replied, "Yes … I will! I love you."

I hung up the phone to a silent car. I explained in as few words as possible what just happened and boarded the plane to St. Mary's. For the 4-hour flight to St. Mary's, I was in my head about so many recurring thoughts I was hung up on. Of all people, I am going to be with Jay for these two weeks. This person, this friend, who I admire and cherish, was not going to be able to provide the strength I would need emotionally to be present for the job I so truly loved. I would have to rely on myself and the connection I have to this program and my grandmother. I created a game plan of how to thrive independently during this time, as well as try to not hold a grudge against Jay for what I viewed as his low emotional sensitivity.

When we landed in the village St. Mary's, I was ready. My plan was comprised of journaling, letter writing, and just embracing all the components of this program, this would lift me and carry me until I could get home. I was confident I could be successful in navigating controversy and disagreement. I was prepared for anything these two weeks could throw at me from my emotions, interactions with Jay, and the program itself.

Then the curve ball: I checked my voice mail. It was not three to five weeks, but three to five hours my grandmother survived in order to speak with me and her brother (the only two of our family that could not be by her bedside). In the time it took me to get to St. Mary's, my rock was gone. As I hung up the phone, I was in disbelief. Jay was there. I didn't have to tell him what happened; he knew. I tried to be tough and just focused on the plan I created in my head, but within minutes that plan was out the window and I lost it.

To my surprise, Jay became everything that I needed in this moment. He picked up the phone and made arrangements for me to get home. I just sat there in disbelief, not only at the loss of my Grams but also at the emotional support, compassion, and empathy my friend was providing for me. We walked back in the rain to our dwelling. I sat on the floor while he made dinner. He created conversation, just asking questions and listening.

From my past experiences with Jay, I figured he would select the bedroom he wanted, set up the place how he saw fit, did some of his rituals and routines he needed and then go into his bedroom. But he didn't. He put that all aside; he was my rock. We played cards, we talked, we slept in the same room, and he comforted me. He handled everything dealing with the program, while preparing for being alone when I left.

I woke up early the next morning, and it was still raining (which was fitting for how I felt). I sat in a chair overlooking the village and river. As I cried, I didn't hear Jay get up, but suddenly I could feel his energy around me. His hands were on my shoulders and he was just there. Anyone who has lost someone close to them remembers that feeling of numbness. I can't remember much of those two days in St. Mary's, but I remember the gratitude that I felt, and still carry with me, for Jay.

He allowed me to tell stories of my Grams. He held me while I cried. He said it was ok. Who was this man before me? It was all about me! Here was someone I hadn't seen before. I underestimated his ability to be there when it was really needed. I knew he was one of my best friends, but in that moment, I really understood how loved I was by him.

PLEASE UNDERESTIMATE ME

Thank you, Jay, for your friendship and your willingness to be the friend I needed at this time. I will continue to push your boundaries, and build your capacity for compassion, empathy – and being an emotional sap like me.

"Be incredulous with your words."

— Mary Weiss

IN THE BEGINNING

In the beginning, God decided to create the world, because he was bored, and men usually do unnecessary things when they are bored. And so God thought, "Why the fuck not?" He picked up his heavenly hooch and got to work on a shapeless, lifeless void: Earth. It's best not to ask questions about that or the dinosaurs. He decided to build the world in seven days because he thought it would be important to give the Babylonians a leg up on their calendar, and he also knew seven would be an important number in Harry Potter.

On the first day, God created the heavens and the earth. The earth was easy for God to literally shit out compared to making the heavens. The heavens, (for all you sleepy scientists) was everything beyond earth and outer space, including heaven itself (for all of you church goers). Making everything match in the perfect shade of white is backbreaking work. God almost didn't finish in under 24 hours on this first day, seeing how he had just invented the concept of time, there was no going back. Starting to feel that hooch, God declared the end of the day, "This is good." No one said otherwise, so he ran with it.

On the second day, God created the sky, figuring with his hangover it wouldn't be so hard. After yesterday creating all those dreamy white clouds, the pearly gates, and all those virgins, building the sky was a piece of cake. He put a put a little extra work into Montana on Day 2 and thought he would balance out the favoritism by short changing their economy and the native people who will live there later. After all, God decided to be a fair and just God while daydreaming on a break. God again, declared to no one but himself that this was good.

On the third day, God created dry land, which was convenient because he was tired of floating weightlessly around all the time. The dry land consisted of one giant piece of land known by heretics as Pangea with a built-in, ticking time bomb underneath it to confuse people later writing the Bible. Pangea came together as quick as two farts before a poop, so God thought, "What about plants?" God went to town on creating every kind of living plant, giving them the ability to reproduce themselves, but no orgasms. God thought plants getting off would be too much. Then he declared to all the unsatisfied plants that this was good.

On the fourth day, God created the stars and the heavenly bodies (not to be confused with the very real place of heaven, that God made all the way back on day one). God created two heavenly bodies, the Sun and the Moon.

God thought, "I need this really complicated yin-yang for a man to tell time with and to worship me all the fucking time." God also thought the Sun and the Moon would be great to confuse countless populations on who or what to worship. I mean, am I right?

On the fifth day, God created all creatures that live in the water. Water was created way back in the day, like four days ago. God also created all the birds of the air and may have created the insects of the air on this day as well. It was unclear which day the flying insects were created because the Bible was made up and was so darn pesky to decipher facts; but who really cares? God decided these airborne creatures, insect or otherwise, will have the ability to perpetuate their species by reproduction. Seeing how God had the seven-year itch in God days, he decided to throw the birds a bone and give them orgasms. God declared to the entire bird kingdom (and possibly the blue-ball flying insects) that this was good and he was fucking killing it!

On the sixth day, God created all the creatures that live on dry land. I know what all you dumpy biologists are thinking: "When did God create amphibians that live on both land and water?" Well, it just so happens that God created amphibians at exactly midnight so as not to disrupt the space time continuum which obviously predates God. Most importantly, this is the day God created Man! God wanted to wait to create Man last so as to establish a sense that everything on this planet was made for him and for him to do whatever he wanted with it, even if what he wanted is to trash the place.

Right before God was about to push the button on the Man-making machine, he said: "Let us make Man in our own image, in our likeness." God spoke to himself like this because God was schizophrenic.

"What a great idea," God said.

"Why thank you, God. Say, I declare you are doing a good job ol' chap."

"I was just going to declare you are doing a good job."

God laughed. God also laughed.

God decided he would make Man look just like himself, because God loved looking at himself in the mirror, especially naked. In fact, Lake Baikal was created (in then Pangea, now Russia) just so God could see a good image of his hot bod.

God placed Man in authority over all the earth and all the living creations he just created because God was already tired of all his new toys and didn't care if someone else played with them. Feeling really tired all of sudden, God commanded Man to reproduce and fill the earth.

"With whom?" the Man yelled back to a gorgeous naked God.

Stunned, God whipped around over his shoulder and said, "Did you say that?"

"No, I didn't say that," God said.

"I said that you dumb shit. And my name is Adam. You made me self-aware, remember?"

Slowly and cautiously God turned back to Man, with an exasperated look on his face, as God finally put it all together. He realized Man needed a female to reproduce because that is how he created anatomy. But being so tired after six long days of being "on", God decided to take a shortcut on making a female and ripped out one of Adam's ribs.

"Ouch! My fucking rib!" Adam yelled out.

"You should have used an anesthetic," God said.

"But we are so tired. We invented pain and suffering; we might as well use it." God said back to himself.

And with a flick, God created Women. Eve (who was self-aware too) said, "I would like to be in authority as well."

God chuckled and said, "That's cute, sugar tits. Put a pin in that and we'll talk in 4,000 years." God is a sexist God.

Eve began to retort back eloquently but was briskly cut off by God and Adam in unison declaring that this was good.

On the seventh day, God could barely open his eyes and get out of bed. Who knew the creator of the universe could succumb to at human understanding of physical exhaustion? God decided to rest on this day for his own health and for labor unions to have something to strive for in the future. Well, that and the ability to tweet the shit out of everything he just created.

And that is how God created the world.

"The only thing constant in the world is change."

Let go. You are not in control nor will you ever be.

STICKER N' PLATE

I sat through hundreds of sermons as a child, either in real church or at school. One in particular sermon, I was the volunteer, hand-chosen out of dozens of stage-hungry[10] students who were chosen to come on stage. This speaker/pastor was making a point about once you sin, the sin sticks to you and you can never get it off. He[11] brought me on stage and pulled out a paper plate and a "Hello my name is" sticker. He stuck the sticker to the plate explaining ad nauseam (even for children) that this sticker represented sin and the plate was our souls. Holding the plate for all to see, he finally got to the point and asked me to pull the sticker off.

Little did he know, I was really good at pulling off stickers. I am a very artistic and this was by no means the first sticker I have pulled off. I began to carefully pull up two of the corners and applied even pressure at just the right angle. Despite this pastor's sweaty fingers' thorough application, my nibble child fingers pulled it up perfectly. We exchanged eye contact mid-pull. My look of smug satisfaction and his of panic that he was going to bomb in front of kids that were one step above being homeschooled.

"Pull faster," he said.

I did not. He jerked the plate to force the speed that was not sustainable for my advanced technique and the sticker ripped. I felt cheated. I know I could have got that sticker off that plate unscathed. It was now his turn to act smug and layout how this just proved his point. But really, the experience of the situation exposes the real lesson here:

Left to oneself, an individual can achieve self-improvement and harmony on their own... that is, until a white Christian man feels threatened and tells you that it is impossible and rigs the game.

Am I right? Or am I right?

---

[10] Church is really just a show. It has all the elements of a show: stage, audience, and a performance. But really it is a shit show, because it is a free show and at 9:00 am on Sunday. No thanks.

[11] It's always a HE.

WISHFUL GIBBERISH

I grew up in the church, in an environment where the group enforces individual beliefs. One of my earliest memories was standing in the middle of a circle of adults speaking in tongues. (Yep, I grew up in that kind of church.) This circle of adults was praying and speaking in tongues and persuading me to join in on the fun. I was to let the Holy Spirit in and let him speak through me. At 5 years old, I was terrified. But I also knew that they only way out of this is to give them what they wanted. I joined in the gibberish. A star was born.

I remember thinking the Holy Spirit was not speaking or compelling me to do anything, but at the same time I didn't want to mess up this cult ritual, so I just faked it. As soon as some nondescript mumbles came out of my mouth, the entranced coven rejoiced and encouraged me to let the Holy Spirit in and to speak through me. I gave them what they wanted; even then I could read a crowd and let them just eat up my 'tongues'.

Not only was I in the church but I also went to my church's K-8 grade school: Bible class four days a week, weird talks and chapel on Fridays, Sunday morning service, and youth group on Wednesday nights. I got my fill of gibberish.

Birthday Spanking

Just to give you an idea of what happens in a small, underfunded Christian school, I want to tell you about how birthdays were celebrated. I was in a 2nd/3rd grade combined classroom. There was a 2nd grader who was having a birthday and her 3rd grade brother was also in the same classroom. Because of her birthday, my teacher wanted to make it special and devote class time to this girl getting her birthday spankings. She took quietly raised hands from students to come to the front of the class and give this girl a spanking with a yard stick. I don't know which was worse: the teacher doing the spanking or auctioning off each spank to the children. This is what class time was devoted to: not math, not science, not even speaking in gibberish, but spankings. The lesson plan for that day was for a 2nd grade girl to come to the front of the classroom, present, and be playfully spanked by her peers.

Hands were raised to volunteer for each spanking correlated to each year this girl had been alive. Seeing how there were only eight spanking slots, they were coveted. Spankings one through seven were gentle wafts using the flat side of a yard stick: light and gay. The last and most precious spanking was between handfuls of eager students in serious danger of waiting till the next birthday to get their public spanking fix. Our teacher lingered a bit too long in deciding which anxious hand raise student would be chosen. But the victor of the last birthday spanking went to her older brother and my friend.

He walked to the front of the class like he won the lottery. His sister looked over her shoulder with hesitation and then made foreboding eye contact with the teacher. With a flick of her eyes, the teacher instructed her to look away and get back in the proper spank-receiving position that all young ladies should know. One last, sweaty, over-the-shoulder look, then heads down. Her brother wound way back with the yard stick high in the air, twisted it to the thin side, and brought it down hard like a blade cutting the air. It was faster and harder than I thought possible for a third grader to accomplish. I remember being surprised the classroom yard stick had not broken. A swing like that would have cut a watermelon in half.

There was a moment of silence and stillness. Then everyone reacted at an alarming volume. The birthday girl screamed and was carried out because she couldn't walk. The class was traumatized. The brother was straight up baffled to what he had done wrong as if spankers one through seven could have easily chosen the same path he did, but merely chose not.

I was not traumatized and looking back, that is the worse part for me. Why wasn't that super fucked up to me? This is the only memory I have from 3rd grade at that school. This is what happens at Christian schools; is this what happens everywhere? It is the sexism of this memory that I wish I had stood up and spoken out against or at least felt that this tradition is horrible and wrong? I did come to the conclusion having a summer birthday (that no one ever came to), that it actually wasn't such a bad thing.

It is the internal misogamy that every man grows up eating, breathing, and living. It, unfortunately, takes self-awareness and an openness to even see it in ourselves. Men, we need to stand up against the sexism and chauvinism that we are spoon-fed because it is fucked up and really if you break it down the joke is on us.

Mr. Fear

My 8th grade teacher was a monster in my life. Mr. Fear had been teaching 8th grade at this school forever. He was a giant creep and because this was a private school, he really did whatever he wanted. He taught history but mainly taught what my parents said was his own opinions.

Mr. Fear was constantly singling me out. Once in computer class, he did not respond to my question because I was using my hands too much while talking. He had me sit on my hands and ask again. Being confused, I didn't respond right away when sitting on my hands and he started making fun of me to the class. He singled me out to draw attention to the gender codes that I was breaking. Maybe he thought that I would fix my effeminate behaviors if he brought public attention to them. He was wrong. [Fancy hand motion]—Or maybe he tried to bring me down out of fear, because he knew I was a stronger person than he was, even at my young age. He probably knew that someday I would be dancing on his grave.

One day, the history lesson was on the signing of the Declaration of Independence. His lecture was based on the significance of what it meant for the men who signed it. He explained at misogynistic length that by signing the Declaration of Independence it meant that the King of England would kill you. By signing this paper, you would be killed by the king. But Mr. Fear went on at length about how death was a noble cost to pay for freedom, how America is the greatest country in the world, and God was a founding father of this country.

After a heavy dose of American Christian propaganda, the real exercise began. He asked the whole class whether or not we would sign the Declaration of Independence? He went through the whole class and each student had to verbally answer the question one at a time. Everyone in my class said, "Yes" they would sign the Declaration of Independence... everyone except me. I said, "NO, I would not sign the Declaration of Independence." [Gasp]

My class was in shock. Immediately I was expected to explain myself. I stated I wasn't going to sign this piece of paper if meant I would be killed. Mr. Fear moved on.

Once class was over and we were filing out of the classroom Mr. Fear pulled me aside and said, "Hey, I am really glad you said that you wouldn't sign the Declaration of Independence. I know that you really would have signed it and that you just wanted to say something different from everyone to make the discussion better. But we both know you would sign it."

At that age, I didn't know how manipulative this was. I thought that he had misunderstood me. I told him, "I would not sign the Declaration of Independence! I would not die for this country or any country." My thinking was the same with all the other Christian-glorified martyr stories as well; why not just lie? Save yourself in the moment. Who cares what this asshole thinks or believes about you?

PLEASE UNDERESTIMATE ME

My teacher thought he could still convince me I was wrong.

He thought that he could change me.

Mr. Fear thought that he could get me to doubt myself.

Mr. Fear was wrong.

He underestimated me and now look at this unpatriotic agnostic that stands before you.

5-DAY CLUBS

My church did these things called 5-day clubs, which were exactly like vacation bible schools. If you don't know what that is, then you're an atheist and are going to hell. Christian teenagers would put on church camps for kids to church at them while being 'churched' at by adults at the same time. We would have them in Portland and road-trip to out-of-town places as well. I was a typical teen who hated my parents and was trying to figure out how to get along with others. I was on fire for The Lord and wanted to give my life to Christ, but as an angsty teen, I also wanted to take it back! So these are the journals from summers from 1999-2001:

[A vision...]

Jesus standing in front of me, standing in a river. The water is pure and cool. The water hits me at the waist, splashes up covering my whole body. Like if you were to throw a cup of water on a watercolor painting. I was there, face-to-face with my savior, Jesus Christ.

June 8th

I got up on time and left on time, but we got outside and we had a flat tire, so I was late a half an hour. So everyone won't shut the fuck up about it.

June 12th

I, Aaron, and Kyle had the coolest conversation about God and how he has changed my life and theirs. We went hiking in Glacier National park and it was okay. There were so many bugs up there. Then it was time to go to bed Aaron and Kyle told fart stories; they were so funny. I grew really close to God these past two weeks.

So, these journals came out of scrapbooks that I took to 5-day clubs. But they also included doodles, observations of others, and mini plays that I wrote. This next mini play is my take on religion.

[Religious Scene]

Jay: There's the atheist...

Atheist: There can't be a God because this whole world is so screwed up! (Runs off screaming)

Jay: Then there's the Mormons...

Mormon: We are the same as Christians... We just have a different name, different books, and totally different contradicting beliefs then Christian. (Gets on bike and rides off stage)

Jay: Then there's the Christians...

Christian: You aren't a member of Pleasant Crest Community Church? Oh...I have to go, I don't communicate with sinners.

Jay: And last there are the Wiccans...

Wiccan: The Devil is cool! And worshipping Satan has nothing to do with why I drink, do drugs, got pregnant...twice, or why I'm 78 pounds because of bulimia and anorexia.

[End Scene]

May 2nd

For the past four or five months, I have hated my dad with a vengeance. I hate him so much.

May 17th

Today was the best day. I had a dream that the church cancelled 5-day clubs next year.

I and Corinne had a re ally deep conversation about bad stuff that we've done recently. Like me smoking pot and her doing something that I am not going to write about because I promised not to tell anyone. But we really connected. I felt so bad because she read my journal and the part where I totally called her a bitch.

May 18th

Okay, Bryce, Sandra, Karen, and I are sitting around and Bryce and I start talking about listening to Bob Marley. And the CD is just getting good when that asshole Ryan starts walking over to the stereo with another CD. I said to him: "Don't change it."

He said: "Don't worry. I won't."

But the fucking asshole went right over there, stopped my CD, took it out and put his crappy MXPX CD in. Ya know, I thought he had changed because he would talk to me like I existed. He just thinks he is so above everyone else. I want to kill him, and beat his rich, preppy, ass. Ahhhhh! I fucking hate him so much. I want to be Christlike, but I can't take this bullshit from a short, rich, asshole.

May 19th

I saw Corinne sitting alone today so I sat down and it was awesome. We got into a great, deep conversation about our frustrations with friends, relationships, sins, God, and this group. Tomorrow is Disneyland, sooooo I'm going to hang out with Corinne all day. This trip, me and Corrie have buds and it's awesome. I'm totally going to hang out with her after this. We stayed up late last night lighting farts.

May 20th

Disneyland! We got up butt early, but it was worth it. We were in line for Splash Mountain and we saw Linda, Sarah T., Kelsey, and Robby. Robby was in a wheelchair so we hung out with them so he could get us on any ride. I stole so much crap today. I stole about 60 dollars of stuff for people. Amy was the most fun to steal stuff with. I and Lesley and Amy just sat down after going on Splash Mountain and talked about our lives and struggles with God.

May 26th

Well…I did it, I smoked pot. Yes, it was fun. We went to this girl's house and I tried the bong, but I couldn't figure it out, so I switched to the pipe. I took a lot of hits but I wasn't doing it right, then they showed me, and I started to drift off to sleep, then suddenly woke up laughing out of control. Then we went to church. I thought everybody would know and my eyes would be red but they weren't. It was really fun, but now I kind of regret not being able to say I've never done any drugs. Tonight I had a breakthrough with God. I gave him my life to do with as he pleases.

June 6th

My dad is such a fag. Why doesn't he like me? I don't know, but I don't care. He thinks that I'm like a Satan child. He thinks that I only hang out with Goths, bad influences, and punks. He and mom want me to go to bed at 10:00. I'm saying it's never going to happen, so give it up. Then after all the fireworks, my Dad opens the door and is like I love you son. And I know that it is totally out of guilt, so that means that apology is kind of a half-assed apology.

(2 Hours Later)

Looking back on that passage I regret it. My dad is not that bad; he does provide. So, oh well.

July 8th

Today started great, there were nineteen kids. Today two of our leaders could not make it so Natalie decided just to invite Amanda to join our group. Amanda is the biggest bitch and I hate her. So we are waiting for the parents to show up and I'm having fun with the kids just goofing around and here comes the bitch freaking out. "We have to go. It's 8 o'clock, come on." So I just told her to shut up. Then the youth pastor comes up to the car and gives us this lecture on what we should do better, how we can improve the club, our job is to lead little kids to Christ, be the leaders not friends. Well, I have a suggestion for him: shove it up your ass.

July 10th

James woke me and Tom up. And he was all get up and dance if you love the lord. And Tom said "I can't" and I said neither can I. Morning wood. At worship, they did this thing where Adam washed everybody's feet and it was awesome. Because like everybody had these big emotional revelations. Even Tom and Taylor had a thing. Taylor started crying. I got nothing. I and James had a huge conversation about God. I don't know anything. Especially about God. I feel so alone.

July 11th

This was my last year for 5-day clubs, and yes I had another bad team, but I had a blast. A great year. Good friends. Learned a lot about God and my walk. They were great times and I'm sad to go but I hope to be a leader someday soon.

Taylor, Tom, and I slept outside and we were talking. Then Taylor threw a booger on me, we wrestled, and then all 3 of us had a big pillow fight in our underwear. At the end, the girls were looking at us from the window, so I mooned them. When Tom fell asleep, Taylor put his used underwear on Tom's face. We stayed up late lighting farts.

THE BIBLE

he Bible is the most farfetched thing I have ever been sold. The only reason anyone buys it is because we are told it is absolute when we are also being taught not to put our fingers in a socket. There is no distinction from vital life lessons and fairy tales, Greek mythology, lullabies or Buzzfeed.

This is how unreasonable and bizarre the Bible is. Let's take Star Wars for this example. The original Star Wars phenomenon happened in the 70s. It is something that a large part of the world knows about, and loves—just like any run-of-the-mill religious text. Since the original movies, there have been more movies, countless official books, even more, unofficial fan-fiction novels, and thousands of miscellaneous posters, toys, branding, and artifacts of Star Wars. Let's take all of that and put into one, giant document.

Then let's conservatively say we have one thousand authors. And then we will have 1,000 editors who are going to improve this one very bloated document. They are going to cut here and cut there—add a section here, add a section there—move things around and put things out of order. They will read legitimate sections of our document, delete it, and then add their version of that section. We just want them to go hog-wild because they know what George Lucas really meant.

Then, again conservatively, let's space the editors out over one thousand years. Some of them will work together in a scrapbooking circle but most will work alone. When we space them out over time, we will be guaranteed to pick up outdated language, laws, mentalities, and ideals of the past; all of these archaic customs and scientific impossibilities are gems we want to keep as a part of our sacred document.

Then after all that, would it read as Star Wars? Would it even make sense?

That is the baseline question: would you regard it as a sacred text, worshiping and following its principles? Would you even read it?

My guess is: hell no. No one would read it. It wouldn't make any sense. It wouldn't look or sound anything like Star Wars. All of the elements that made Star Wars a global phenomenon and a treasured and loved story wouldn't have survived what the Bible went through.

So why does anyone have any credit in the Bible? Growing up it dawned me that the New King James Version of the Bible has this blatant flaw in the name; this is King James' version of the Bible. A rich white dude from the past benevolently gave us his take on how the Bible should sound. He wanted (needed?) to take it in a new direction, and knew more than all those before him. When Bible lovers talk and get backed into a corner on huge plot holes in Christianity (#plotholes [see below examples]) and end with the Bible being their proof, I want to blow up a Dead Sea Scrolls!

EXAMPLE A

I once had a Christian youth pastor tell me God put the dinosaur bones in the earth with the appearance of age to test our faith. If that is true, the creator of the universe with infinite knowledge of existence beyond human understanding is playing a trick on us. That's fucked up.

EXAMPLE B

A friend told me when I came out to them, just like Peter in the Bible, God has given me a thorn in my side (for life apparently) for me to rise above. Being attracted to men since birth was a pesky ol' thorn in my side for me to overcome, like swearing or biting your nails, or maybe a genetic disorder that you were born with. This "thorn" could have been a gambling addiction or MS. I guess I am lucky it's just dicks. God is good, I guess.

EXAMPLE C

Here is a doozy. If the Bible is real, then God created Satan. If there was nothing outside of this creator's scope, then God 100% had to create Satan just to fuck with us. It would be like if a principal recruited a horrendous bully to take up residence in their school. The principal needs a bully so people know who is nice, who is worthy of worship, who should be followed like a brainless sheep... oh and who should be given money. The bully character is needed also so God can come in and save the day (or, not save the day for some deeper moral lesson). Sometimes the principal will just let the bully traumatize all of us forever, it would seem, so that when he does save the day, the applause and thank-you cards will be that much better. According to the Bible, we are waiting for God to come down and kick the devil's ass, right? Why are we waiting? Couldn't God just do it now? Oh, but that would ruin the sequel, The Book of Mormon.

But hey I shouldn't be so harsh because look at the Bible now! Not too shabby with 3.9 billion copies sold. Eat your heart out, Star Wars.

"Science is constantly proved all the time. If we take any fiction and any holy book and destroyed it, in a 1,000 years that wouldn't come back just as it was. But if we took every science book and ever fact, in a 1,000 years they would all be back because all the same tests would be the same results." —Ricky Gervais

"The fair comes once a year."

I hate when people say "that's not fair" because the world is not fair; the world is a cruel place except for once a year.

BETTY SHOVER

Growing up with a stay-at-home mother, it was very rare to have a babysitter for an evening—and unheard of to be left somewhere overnight—that was, until my parents left my sister and me to be babysat while they went whitewater rafting. They dropped us off at the Shovers' house, which was a family we were close with. The Shovers had eight daughters. The Shovers had daughters for days. The Shover residence was an epicenter for estrogen ruled by the Moon and Mother Gaia. This thriving womb of femininity was the classic case of the father wanting a son, not giving up, and not taking a hint from the Mother Goddess.

The plan was for my parents to drop us off at the Shovers in morning, go whitewater rafting all day and then pick us up the following morning. As a five- or six-year-old, this was the longest I had ever been away from my parents, and I wasn't having any of it. I threw the biggest fit of my life. Screaming, flailing, kicking, crying… I remember clutching onto my mother and being ripped away so she could get in the car to drive away. My mother recalls, as a mother, it was really hard to get in the car and drive away—but she still did it. (Thanks.)

I had no plan to stop throwing a fit and I just kept it up. Betty Shover, the Shovers' matriarch, decide the best way to cure me of my fit was to viciously spank me. My parents spanked me and I don't have any qualms about it, but no one else had ever spanked me. This was unfathomable that another adult would punish me in this manner. I could not comprehend another hand, belt, or paddle wielded by a non-blood relation violating my sweet butt cheeks.

Betty Shover bent me over her left knee, put her right leg over my legs, dug her elbow in between my shoulder blades, exposed my bare ass, and just spanked the shit out of me. This was all before 9:00 am. I took offense to that spanking and quietly cried about it for a while. Betty came in and out of the room where I was sulking to make fun of me and belittle me, literally adding further insult to injury.

Out of boredom and a whole day ahead of me with the Shovers, I begrudgingly moved on to make the best of the situation. In the afternoon, a daughter my age started playing hide-and-seek in the house. She hid and I just couldn't find her. I looked everywhere to no avail, so I just kind of gave up.

One of the older daughters was watching TV in the living room, so I slumped down to watch TV. Next to the TV, there was an open doorway going down the hall to the bathroom and the parents' room. Out of the corner of my eye, I saw a flash go by the open doorway going towards the parents' room. It was a like a lightning bolt in my brain. That flash was the hidden daughter and she was now sneaking in the parents' room. I had her!

I jumped up off the couch, zipped across the living room, through the doorway, and without any warning, busted open the door to the parent's room. It was not the daughter. It was the Mom, Betty Shover, in the middle of the room facing me completely naked. Turns out, she had just taken a shower down the hall. She had one leg in her panties and working on getting her second leg into her underwear.

I just remember looking up at her big dumb face and then looking down at her big hairy vagina and thinking, "What is that? Weird." This was the first time I had ever seen a vagina. In my life, I don't see a lot of vaginas (if you know what I mean). In shock, Betty Shover let go of her underwear to point while yelling, but her second leg got caught in the underwear and she fell, HARD. There I was, five or six years old, watching her just eat it on her cement bedroom floor and thought she probably broke a tooth.

I immediately shut the door, ran upstairs, and hid. I hid for a long time just thinking so many thoughts. I thought that it was quite fitting that Betty Shover got hurt, I did enjoy that, I thought about the vagina I just saw. But what I thought most about was men. In this sea of women and daughters, I remember thinking that men were really cool.

GILBERT BLYTHE

My parents enrolled me into private Christian school growing up, which meant there was only one small class for each grade. There is a side effect when you go to a private middle school which many people don't know: you, as a student, are in the same room with the same 24 students all day, every day. This experience was compounded because this was also my family's church, the youth group I was forced/wanted to attend, and pretty much my whole world. Spending every day with someone is not uncommon in the workplace; it can be just fine or horrible. But at least in the workplace, you are getting paid fat stacks and you get to go home. When you are a child in a private school, every class, every activity, every lunch, break, weekend, retreat, and fart is in the company of the same fucking people. When you are a child in a private school, you live at work.

I developed an enemy in my class out of jealousy; his name was Anthony. I remember a classmate responding to my negative comment about Anthony by saying, "You're just jealous, Jay," and I instantly knew she was right. I hated Anthony. He had red hair, but that is not why I hated him. I hated him because he was good at everything. He was a top student and star athlete (neither of which described me). He was better at drawing then I was, and he was funnier than me. These cut deep because drawing and being funny were the only cards I was playing with at the time and for him to be better in these two areas was quite discouraging.

In the small pool of my Christian classroom, he was much higher on the social totem pole, and I hated him from my spot near the ground. The bastard even went through puberty before me. I remember he raised his hand for a question and I spied a fresh frock of orange armpit hair. My jealousy seethed about that moment, while I stared at my own inadequate naked armpits in the mirror for hours later that night.

I was pretty open about my hate of Anthony at school, which nobody really addressed or tried to stop. In a Bible class video I made, there was a cutaway commercial where I did an impression of Anthony[12], my impression mocking him for collecting and using sample bottles of perfume (again, with no adult intervention). Morality is really subjective in the church. Anthony did not like my impersonation and afterward, timidly shoulder checked me while filing out of class. That was all the reaction I got from Anthony; us Christian kids are real tough.

[12] Commercial breaks were all the rage in kid homemade video's shot in the '90s.

After 8th grade graduation, public high school came. We ended up going to the same high school, but my hatred of Anthony didn't matter anymore. There were new people and new groups of friends. My whole world opened up when I went to a public school. So many different points of view, new styles, and opinions... it really was an awaking from what felt like an inescapable cycle. How torturous, I really wanted to be David Bowie but then was forced into thinking that I wanted to be stuck living in a cookie cutter.

Shortly into my high school career, my family moved from the little town of Boring, OR (again, a real town; Google it if you don't believe me...) to the exciting suburb of Gresham, OR. Throughout the entire process of my family buying our new home, it never occurred to me to look around and check out the other houses. It wasn't until we were picking up the keys that my attention was drawn to the house directly across the cul-de-sac where a proud sign reading "The D's..." stood. My enemy had become my neighbor. NOOOO! However, my initial feeling of dread quickly melted when I realized I could prank my enemy within the comfort of my own neighborhood.

Highlight Reel of Anthony's Neighborly Torment:

The Pizza Paparazzi

From the comfort of my parents' living room looking onto Anthony's driveway, I called every delivery pizza place in town on behalf of Anthony. All six large pepperonis arrived within two minutes of each other. Pizza Hut would be leaving as Domino's was pulling in. Drivers exchanged sentences like, "It's a prank. Don't go in. Oh, you have acne too.[13]" Being able to watch the whole prank from just across the cul-de-sac was quite rewarding; there is nothing like seeing the fruits of one's labor.

The Gnome Hunt 'n' Dump

Gnome hunting-and-dumping was a practice I worked on a lot in my teenage years. The idea was to scour dozens of suburban lawns blotted with retirement-idle hands and steal ornaments, such as flags, flamingos, flower pots, benches, cement geese, etc... over the span of the evening. This was such a good time for teenage bonding and giggle-fest-NW. Once the booty was gathered, we kept what we wanted and dumped the rest in our enemy's front yard. It was imperative to dump in silence to avoid being caught by a robe-clad mom. (Should you try this and are discovered by said mom, avoid

---

[13] Or so I imagined.

panicking, driving erratically, and smashing your getaway truck into the neighborhood communal mailbox. Lessons learned.)

The Panty Massacre

This was a take on the classic prank 'Forking a Lawn[14].' If you don't know what 'Forking a Lawn' is, then you never went to Youth Group and are going to Hell. The idea by the teenage collective was is to step on the knives, concealing them in the ground until someone mows the lawn in which the lawn mower would quickly discover them to hilarious effect. All ideas are good ideas in a teenage prank brainstorm, but the limit was not killing anyone. The creative direction went to using the real metal butter knives to stab something our victim would not want to touch. [Enter, stolen panties from Goodwill.] We stole as many panties and butter knives that would fit in my bag, which was a lot.

Under the cover of darkness, we went to work on stabbing panties in Anthony's lawn. We heard a dog bark, and a porch light flicked on. We dove into the bushes just in time for a person to come out and yell, "Shut up, dog! There's no one there." Yeah, dog, there was no one there. Meanwhile, the dog could hear more than all humans involved in this story. We finished stabbin' those panties. In the morning the dog was heard to have said, "I told you there was someone there."

Let's fast forward to my early adulthood. I went through a phase of a lot of self-reflection where I started thinking about many of the poor choices I made as a teenager. There were so many! Often people came up to me and told me stories of the awful things I had done and I have no memory of it. Some of these stories were lighthearted, fun things and most of those I don't remember either. This still happens in my life today; I think it is the plight of an improviser. But most of the stories of Teenager Jay came back to me as awful, horrendous: a reflection of a person I didn't want to be. I would not want to hang out with that person. I was a bully. How did that happen?

When I reflected on all of these stories and all of "enemies" I had tortured, I kept coming back to how much I hated Anthony. The question was, why did I hate this dude? What had he done to me to cause me to spend so much of energy hating him? All he had every done was be in my class, be my neighbor, and in general was more talented than me. He had never

[14] Instead of plastic forks, use metal knives.

wronged me…?

That was when I had an epiphany: I didn't hate Anthony. I had a GIANT crush on him!

Growing up, I watched other people have crushes all around me, and was frustrated while waiting for a crush to happen to me. But in fact, it was happening to me the whole time. I grew up in an environment where I could not process having a crush on another boy.

It was just like in *Anne of Green Gables* when Gilbert Blythe (and I am Gilbert in this scenario) super likes "Anne with an E" but doesn't know what to do, except to call her "carrots." It was just like that except my redhead was a boy. And we didn't end up together. And I didn't end up getting typhoid fever.

This happens all the time in our society, and I was no exception. How many times have we seen the most outspoken homophobic dude later comes out as gay? At this point it is cliché. I know deep down I am gay, but our culture, society, church and family are overtly (or covertly) telling us this is wrong. Therefore, as a way to be seen as straight, we become the bully and the strongest proponent of hate: not an intrinsic ideology to any person. No one will think I'm gay because I am calling people fags and gender-policing anyone who is just a bit more of a fruit then I am.

The real evil in this cycle is not protecting how we are seen by others, but how we see ourselves. And what a clever prank: to get the group you hate to hate themselves first. This will force them to hate others that are like themselves. The cherry on the hate cake is: your original victim will end up doing your bullying for you. It's genius. But now we know, the world is changing and we can escape the cycle.

I am sorry for all of the awful things I did when I was a teenager. I wish that I had not perpetuated hate to hide who I am. I wish I was raised by a more enlightened culture and by atheist parents. Moreover, I'm most sorry I missed out so many possible teenage make-out sessions. Damnit.

60/40

There is something that you need to know about gay men: we can smell each other. There is something about it; it's like a sixth gay sense. Now, there is nothing more alluring then the smell of what I like to call a "60/40.": that is, a guy who is 60% straight and 40% gay. They hold onto that 60% hard, but that 40% has to get out sometime. All the crazy fundamentalist Christians talk a lot about the gay agenda and one of their points is that we are trying to turn straight people gay. Now that one is 100% true. I'll give them that one.

Being a 60/40, the 60% is in charge most of the time and keeps the 40% hidden away, always bullying him to stay out of sight. But the 60% cannot be vigilant all the time; it has to sleep sometimes. And that is when the 40% comes out and lets her hair down. Those are the moments where the 100% gay men are waiting for like alligators waiting for the wilder beasts to cross the river.

A while ago I did a lot of improv performing with a 60/40. He was handsome and had all the classic signs of a 60/40; was still dating his high school sweetheart, she was into musical theater, he was into musical theater, they moved out to Portland together; all the signs were there. Plus, he had a six pack; straight guys just don't have six packs. If you are a dude with a six pack, you're gay. If you are reading this and you are a straight dude with a six pack, and you are thinking, "Hey! I am not gay!"—well, you might have some self-reflection to do.

This 60/40 and I performed together many times. Since this was improv, (and you're just making it up on the spot) our scenes together would get real gay, real fast. Somehow we were always playing a gay couple or exaggerated gay characters; even if I established that I was playing a women character, he would not hear it and start talking about how we were super-gay in love. Being improvisers, we'd trained ourselves remain unfiltered: *let it fly, don't think*... This can be very telling of what is in one's mind. The saying is: "A drunk man's words are a sober man's improv scenes." So true.

We had this flirtatious relationship for about a year. Prior to one of our shows, he came up to me and said, "Hey Jay, my girlfriend is out of town all weekend. I have the place to myself. What are you doing after the show? We should hang out." All I heard was, "My girlfriend is out of town" and then I stopped listening. Game on!

After the show, the whole cast went to the local bar for drinks and 60/40 and I were on the Sexy Time Express. There were green lights everywhere.

I casually mentioned I would love to smoke some weed right about then and he replied, "Oh, I have some weed at my house. Let's go smoke some." (Two of my favorite things: Weed and *your house*.) We started to leave and I heard a dangerous voice behind us. The enemy of all 60/40 moments: a hot, straight woman. "Are you guys going to smoke weed?"

We turned around to just in time for a slow motion Baywatch hair flip performed by this particular hot, straight woman who had previously been undetected by my scans.

60/40 stated, "Yeah, we are going to smoke weed at my house. Do you want to come with us?" Through gritted teeth, I added, "…Yeah, do you want to come with us?"

As we loaded up my bike on his car, I tried to I shake off a feeling that this night was now ruined, and forced myself to take a new stance. I thought, *"This is fine. We'll smoke some weed. The hot girl will leave and then I will get to the Lord's work and have a gay ol' time."* Everything was still on track.

We arrived. We smoked. All the fun energy left. We could not keep a conversation going, nor find anything to do but end up trying to play Apples to Apples on the floor. There were only three of us, so it really sucked. This evening was going south fast. The hot girl kept saying, "I am so tired."

I kept thinking, *"Well, if you are so tired why don't you just leave?"* Then I realized this whole time I was waiting for her to leave, she was waiting for ME to leave. We were both on the hunt. Well, two would play this game. I jumped on the tired game to try to squeeze her. I started yawning. She yawned too, but with a cute collapse on his shoulder. I rolled over and with a good long stretch. She rolled over as if an ocean wave just splashed her on her perfect amount of cleavage. All her years of honed feminine tricks had made her too strong. I couldn't compete with that. It was getting so late and so boring that I gave in.

I announced I was going to bike home. This immediately energized the room! Everyone was up and alive. 60/40 full of energy told me that he was going to drive me home as he promised he would. Game changer.

All hope was not lost and I was back in the game. But all too quickly, the emperor struck back and the hot girl chimed in, "I'll take Jay home for you." Nooooooo!

60/40 refused because he promised that he would take me home. But Hot Girl was too strong and she wouldn't take no for an answer.

"You work in the morning. I don't. Let me do this for you."

Classic move: setting yourself up for the next time the girlfriend was out of town. 60/40 refused again. Hot Girl rebutted, "His bike can fit in my car. He lives in SE; I live in SE. I want to do this for you."

Damn it, that made a lot of sense. Damn you, hot straight girl! She was so insistent and her logic made too much sense to be denied. I was helpless.

60/40 and I walked down the dark and gloomy stairwell from the second floor apartment. We forlornly walked across the dark street to his car where my bike was locked up. As we were pulling down my bike, we looked at each other for a moment, wondering what happened to the night we were promised. His 40% said, "Damn it!" My 100% said, "DAMN IT!" The 60% said, "Phew, that was a close one, Bro."

We loaded my bike begrudgingly into the hot girl's car. We said good-bye to 60/40. As soon as her door was closed all pretense and feminine wiles dropped. She lit up a Paul Mall cigarette like a trucker and turned to me to say, "Don't you just think is he is so hot?" I looked her right in her dumb face and said, "Yeah, I do. Now take me home, bitch."

"Get out of family what you want to get out of family."

— Jose Guadarrama Torrés

Hearing this changed my life. Some people have biological connections to their family and a shit ton of people don't. Most of my friend family is closer to me than anyone I am kin with.

FATHER-SON EMBARRASSMENT

Freshman year of high school, I was talking on a chorded phone in the kitchen of my house with my best friend Taylor about all the happenings of my water polo team. It was around nine at night on a weekday, and my father was putzing around in his robe before heading to his room for the night. I started talking about an upper-classman on the varsity team and even though my dad was in and around the kitchen, I took a risk and just said, "Jaren Castdon is such a prick." My dad immediately halted his putzing, turned to me and said, "What did you say?"

"I said Jaren Castdon is a prick."

"Do you know what that means?

"...."

"That means your pee-pee."

Right when he said pee-pee, he slightly kicked his leg out and quickly pointed to his own junk through the loose robe.

Time stood still. I was in shock. Taylor on the phone kept talking unknowingly in my ear.

Almost immediately after "pee-pee" left my father's mouth, he regretted his juvenile and odd word choice. My facial expression of embarrassment for myself and him made it undeniable. His will to punish and hold me accountable for using foul language was overrun by his self-defeating word choice. For a grown man in his late 40's, to utter "pee-pee" to his teenage son in a moment of anger would not allow him to save face. He broke eye contact and scurried off to bed straining to salvage a morsel of dignity.

I interrupted Tyler to tell him my father had used the term "pee-pee." We laughed at my father so foolishly not knowing that what goes around, comes around.

Fast forward eight years:

I purchased a new bed frame when I was 23 years young, and I asked my father to come help me pick it up and assemble it because that is what I'd deemed his job as my father to be. We got the bed frame (thank you, IKEA) and brought it back to my house. Once the new frame was put together and ready to receive the box spring and mattress, my father and I saddled up to lift the mattress. We lifted and shuffled over carrying the mattress. That was the moment when embarrassment rained down upon me. Freshly exposed to the light of day was some gay erotica I had left under my mattress and forgot to remove.

Time stood still. We both saw it, but we were both holding a heavy awkward mattress. We had to continue holding and moving the mattress for which seemed like an hour across my bedroom. Once the mattress was down, I scampered over to the box spring of filth, grabbing the erotica to be hidden from view but not from my father's mind. That was the most embarrassed I have ever been in my life. I didn't have the luxury of scampering off to bed to save face like my father did eight years earlier because we still had a bed to put together. I'd like to imagine that my father had a good laugh with someone about this moment—but he probably just prayed about it.

MORTIFIED

Like most teenagers during their high school years, I desperately wanted to make an impression and be noticed by my teachers and classmates. By my senior year, I wanted to be in every yearbook photo. I wanted to win Mr. Barlow, our local male beauty pageant. But most of all, I really wanted the lead in our spring play, *Fools*, which was my last chance to show everyone how talented I was. Well, my senior year had some disappointments and I felt wronged, which basically came out as bitter, envious anger. I couldn't take out on my parents or teachers, so I took it out on my arch nemesis, the good ol' all-American boy next door. (Let's call him "Boy next door.") Being really into pranking people, he was the main focus of my attention. So instead of being the class clown (which I desperately wanted to be voted), I was really more of the class prick.

The following are diary entries from my senior year in high school:

August 17:

Today is my Golden Birthday; I am 17 on the 17th. It's crazy. I'm old. I'm having a lot of fear and experiencing a lot of weird feelings.

August 21:

Today was so cool. I went to Mike's house, where there was a bunch of people. We then drove around throwing water balloons at people walking. After that, we were walking in the park and there was these people's pool. Me, Tom, and Barry went and jumped in it, and then ran away.

September 5:

The first day of senior year. Man, I'm having such a good life right now. Bought Incubus tickets.

October 13:

Today I got FUCKED. Taylor came over and we went to Nate's house. We got eggs and, of course, I got stuck driving. Basically, we got caught by a cop and my mom caught me. My life is so fucked. So far, I've lost my parents' trust and the Incubus concert.

November 23:

Work is getting increasingly more difficult. Christmas bonus is coming up and, goddamn it, I've been working at that shithole (and for that unibrow bastard, Darren) for too long, so I better get a good chunk of the pie.

November 24:

Today I've come to the realization that Thanksgiving is the worst of all holidays; in fact, it really sucks ass. This weekend I sat on my ass, and did nothing but sit on my ass.

December 9:

My parents really suck ass lately.

December 17:

I've just discovered that Christmas is really going to suck ass.

February 6:

I feel totally confident going in for tomorrow's audition for the spring production of *Fools* with Viva, my drama teacher.

I stole a whole bunch of stuff today. I went to the basketball game (Gresham vs. Barlow) and put a stink bomb and this stinky hair shit all over Boy Next Door's air vents of his truck. Yes!

Shockingly, I was very involved in our local church youth group. Every year we went on a retreat called "Dunes" at the Oregon Coast. Basically, it was just a free pass for me to prank more kids and get into more mischief. But don't worry; I still had my great attitude!

February 17:

Dunes has been 50/50 good/bad. We've had a lot of fun doing crap, but everyone blames me for everything. Benny talked to me sternly, which is bullshit because I haven't done anything. They're putting me as the ringleader. This retreat is freaking boring. I'm surrounded by people I hate and idiots. Last night we threw a bag of whipped cream right in a kid's face. It was funny, but he freaked out and cried like a little girl.

February 20:

I'm tired of stealing stuff. I'm sick of myself as a human being. I hate Boy Next Door.

February 28:

Stealing has become a real problem for me. Survivor is on again. Yes!

March 5:

I tried out for *Fools* today and if Viva shafts me again, then I swear, I'm going to tell her off. I really want a lead. It's my damn senior year.

March 6:

Today I was not cast in Fools. No one good was cast either, so I pulled the cast list off the wall and ripped it up twice.

3 things piss me off:

1. I was shafted for a lead or even a part.
2. All the seniors were shafted.
3. To top it off, the cast is full of talentless people. Viva can lick my crotch.

Tonight I wrote all over Boy Next Door's window with candle wax. It was great, but I got caught. I am full of anger. I hope he spends a long time cleaning off his car.

March 7:

Viva is a stupid whore.

March 12:

Our vice principal is a dirty whore. He gave me a 2nd period in-house suspension. Viva and the Vice Principal can take turns sucking my dick.

Clearly, I was really angry at my drama teacher, Viva, and our vice principal, who didn't seem to appreciate my creativity and talent. Soooo, of course, I took that rage and channeled it to....unsuspecting Boy Next Door. One of the pranks that I am most proud of involved me calling a gravel company and ordering a dump truck filled with gravel to be delivered early one morning C.O.D. (Cash on Delivery) to Boy Next Door's house.

April 24:

Well, the whole gravel Boy Next Door thing totally worked. They called the cops and I'm busted. First, my parents were saying I lost my car, going to be riding the bus. But I'm keeping my car; I can drive to school and work. So basically, I have to pay the truck fees, like a hundred bucks. Big whoop. I have a mediation with Boy Next Door and our parents but am grounded until that mediation. My life is so full of scandals these days. I always win with my parents. SUCKERS!

May 5:

My dad is so stupid and annoying. He is freaking out about this gravel thing. Shut up!

May 23:

The senior banquet was tonight. Trying to find a place to sit was hard because there were so many freaks I didn't want to sit by. I did not get voted class clown. Man, I hate that son of a bitch Michael who go it. Prom King, Mr. Barlow, and now my class clown. Motherfucker! All these people at my school fucking suck!

May 26:

My parents are the lamest asses in the whole world. I hate them every waking fucking moment. My dad told me that I couldn't go on a road trip with Taylor. Fucker! Then he offers to go with us. Yeah, fucking right! No one wants to go on a road trip with your stupid, Bible, psycho lame ass! Fuck you.

June 1:

Today we went gnome hunting until 2:00 am. We stole: flag, cement boy/wheel barrel sculpture, graduation goose, huge clay sun, welcome sign, flower windmill, pink flamingo, pants, and moved Kim's bird bath across the street. Good times.

June 6:

Graduation!

I was bored as all hell. I was itching to get out of there. The graduation ceremony was actually very quick. Outside the coliseum was a crazy amount of people. The senior all-night party was a great thing to do. We had tons of poker tables, race cars, sumo wrestling, and good food. It was at the Double Tree Hotel and I came home at 6:30 am.

June 9:

Yesterday, Michelle and I threw tampons with ketchup on the Mormon building. It was fun. Then I came home and had a huge fight with my mom, met up with Travis, and smoked some weed.

June 19:

Today I got arrested for stealing Chinese food at Safeway.

July 7:

Yesterday I bought some emergency weed. I keep it locked up in my safe. Weed is bad. What am I going to do with my life!? I spent last night at Taylor's house. I got more stoned than ever before. It was fun though. Weed is bad!

July 18:

Today I worked and Eric smoked me out with his weed on our lunch. After work, I went to Dana's house, fell asleep on her couch and peed my pants.

August 3:

Lately, I've been smoking a lot of weed. I feel sick. I've become wrapped up in weed culture. I need family right now. I'm at a point in my life where I'm deciding where I will go and what I will do. I miss friends and people I once knew. What a scary and confusing state.

August 30:

Court Date! (Chinese food)

Today I got up at 8:00 AM, went garage sale shopping with Mom, and then went to court. Acted professional and the judge liked me, said I'm going to let this go with a warning. Awesome. My life is great.

"Other people's success is not your failure."

I trip on this constantly. It is a trap to compare yourself to others because there will always be someone better, smarter, faster than you. Focus on yourself, your accomplishments, and your own drive. You will never be David Bowie, no one will so don't compare you to a God. Don't compare yourself to your peers either and don't be bitter if they get a break. Yours is coming.

JAY'S STORY

Guest Chapter by Keith Flewelling (Jay's Father)

I would characterize Jay as a man unto himself. Although social and definitely not a loner, entertainment for Jay was not dependent of other participants. On many occasions I would spy him caught up in an adventure, in full regalia, commanding the backyard all by himself or perhaps with the dog, to play the dragon role opposite the brave and fierce knight. His life was full and mostly contained within himself.

When involved with groups, Jay was often with the girls rather than the boys. I think he found the girls more intellectually challenging than the boys. Boys his age were typically all about sports. Jay was not all consumed with sports like other boys his age. Make no mistake though: Jay was not a girly-boy. In fact, in one playground incident, Jay gave another boy a bloody nose probably responding to being teased about his long hair (which was not in style at the new school).

Intelligent and positive, pleasant, funny, comfortable on stage and in the spotlight: this is the Jay I know. At times Jay can be compassionate and empathetic. I remember a conversation he had with his grandfather during the last months of his life. Jay was trying to connect with the ailing former missionary and pastor by talking to his grandfather about how Jay was, in essence, doing the same things as his grandfather had done. Jay was following in his grandfather's footsteps: providing entertainment, telling stories and messaging social themes very similar to what his grandfather had done from the pulpit every week. Jay's grandfather did not see it that way (but that's another story for another time).

Like all humans and superheroes, Jay does have a dark side that comes to the foreground when triggered. During the high school years, a running battle developed between Jay and another boy. By this time, Jay was over six feet tall and over 200 pounds. Needless to say, he did not cower away from confrontation. More likely, he enjoyed his physical stature, using it to assert dominance. As alluded to, Jay had a touch of arrogance, a highly developed sense of justice and retribution, and was intolerant of certain groups of people. These are the dark attributes that led to the stories to follow.

I was never privy to the whole story and I am sure there are parts of the story, on both sides, that will never be known. As I recall, it all started when Jay became obsessed with a "lesser being" named Bill Watto. I far as I know, the first missile launch was the toilet-papering of the Flewelling home. This act was performed in the middle of the night under cover of darkness: an obvious act of outright cowardice. To my amazement, this sent Jay into an absolute hysteria about the "outrageous and unwarranted attack on a man's castle."

The retaliation attack was less juvenile; it involved research, planning and tactical implementation. At an opportune time, Jay (and perhaps his friend, Tyler) made their way to a grocery store, far away from the Flewelling home or close to Bill's home. The team of two chose random cars in the parking lot, leaving a small piece of paper under the windshield wipers. On the pieces of paper was the message, "*I'm sorry I accidentally hit your car. Please call me at 555-1212 to get my insurance information.*"

Of course, the phone number on the note was Bill's home phone number. And even though there was no damage to the cars, we were told later that Bill's parents received several calls before they understood what was happening.

This prank did not have the desired effect, nor did it satisfy the need for justice, apparently. There we were, Jay's mother and I, enjoying a peaceful end of the day at home following hours of yard work on a pleasant sunny spring day. There was a loud knock at the front door (not a common occurrence at our quiet suburban cul-de-sac home). Standing politely on front step was a County Sheriff's Deputy. I knew immediately the next conversation would undoubtedly be about my son. Sure enough, the first inquiry came...

'Do you know Jay Flewelling?"

"Yes, he's our son...what has he done now?"

It turns out Jay had arranged a delivery to the home of Bill's family. This was no small delivery; it was a dump truck full of gravel to be dumped in front of the garage at the stated address. Payment for the delivery would be made on receipt of the goods. The deputy went on to explain that Sid's mother was home at the time and managed to stop the delivery before any of the contents were dumped. With full knowledge of the ongoing rivalry between her son and Jay, she correctly identified Jay as the culprit and filed a complaint with the Sheriff's Office. The non-delivery, dry-run charge from the gravel company was $125. Of course, Bill's mother and the Deputy were strongly intimating that the Flewelling family should bear the cost of this near-disastrous practical joke.

Being the good parents that we were, we agreed to cover the charges. When confronted with the outcome of his activity, Jay was contrite and repentant. I suppose in retrospect this was one of many times I experienced Jay's acting abilities. We did all the actions and ranted all the things parents are supposed to do; we demanded Jay should pay the charges from the gravel company and grounded him for who knows how long. He, of course, accepted the consequences and appeared humbled and rehabilitated.

Perhaps five or six years later, I attended one of Jay's comedy shows. It was the first time I attended any of his shows and this one had a higher-quality production feel to it. During Jay's section of the show, he detailed the story of the gravel delivery episode from his perspective. Jay's punch line to the story: "It was the best $125 dollars I have ever spent!"

At the end of the show, Jay told the audience that his father was in the audience and conveyed his love. That made it all worthwhile for me. Love you, Jay.

COMING OUT

I have never "come out" to my parents. I don't believe in "coming out". I just don't think that it is a thing that should be that important. No one busts into a room and proclaims "Announcement everyone: I…like strawberries!" No one does that because it doesn't matter to anyone if you like or don't like strawberries. That is how it should be about what genitals you want in your mouth.

My parents aren't stupid; they know what's up. We just don't talk about it. It is like *Midnight in the Garden of Good and Evil*, where I'm Kevin Spacey (dapper and murderous) while my parents are his sweet southern mother who chooses to sit outside the courtroom.

There was one time we did talk about my sexuality when I was twenty years young. I came home to find a printed-out copy of an e-mail to a friend on my bed. I had left my open e-mail up on the family computer. Although there were some incriminating sentences in that e-mail, nothing was overtly convicting. The next day the last Harry Potter book came out and I spent all day in my room, reading and ignoring my parents. I was scared to talk to them. I was ashamed. As much as I wish I wasn't or had been smarter in how I reacted to my parents' detective work, I was petrified. It had been a year where I was militant about who I was and would stand up to people regularly; for all that bravado in the world, I was cowering at home in fear of my parents.

Part of the reason I did this was that I was raised by a really white family. White people don't talk about anything real. I have never seen my parents argue in front of me. Never. There were barely any disagreements even that my parents ever let me in on. The huge downside of that attitude is not being able to handle it when life gets too real.

I read Harry Potter all day like it was my job, only sneaking out of my room to go to the bathroom once (which was the most nerve-racking choice I have ever made). When I couldn't avoid them anymore, we sat down and we talked in the early evening.

My parents were out of their minds. They deduced I was in a relationship with my friend who I had e-mailed. They thought right under their noses, in their house, we had the gayest of love affairs. All of their evidence was scattered, and patched-together instances proved their case; they sounded like chemtrail conspiracy theorists. They e-mailed my friend to declare to him that the "gig was up", and to leave their son alone. Everything they brought up was misconstrued and wrong. At the time I was certainly "out", but everything they were sighting was crazy talk. I will never forget my father saying, "You should have told us. We could have gotten you therapy."

I could not believe he said that. My dad was actually talking about conversion therapy! Despite what he morally felt about being gay, I never questioned my father's intelligence until that moment; how could my educated and well-read father really believe in something as silly and scary as conversion therapy? After all the evidence, my mother "Sherlock Homles-ed" it together and laid out in front of me, and asked if I was a homosexual. If that was the case, they would not support me; I would have to move out of the house and they would not continue to pay for college.

When it was my turn for rebuttal, I responded that my personal life was none of their business. I told them this would last time we would ever talk about this and I was not gay.

I lied.

I lied right to their faces and it felt great. I had just finished community college, about to move out of my parents' house for the first time, and was on the eve of transferring to Portland State University. A whole new world was about to open up for me. Just like the signing of the Declaration of Independence, why not stay alive and just lie? So, lie is what I did. And let me tell you: every term they paid my tuition at PSU, it felt fucking great.

They never brought up my sexuality again. Every once in a while my mother would comment on pretty a waitress serving us lunch and would wait for my reaction to her sly statement. The most reaction she ever got was a distracted, "I guess… anyway, Mom, what I was saying about improv…"

There is a big push to come out and to be proud and I believe in that for sure—but more than that, I believe in being smart. There was no way that I was going to give up my full ride scholarship with the Flewelling Foundation. My parents instilled in me that I would be going to college, and for that brainwashing, in my mind, they were obligated to pay for it no matter how gay I was. Lying about who you are is cowardice, and sometimes I wish I had been bold, but when it came down to it, I would rather be a coward than have a mountain of student loans. All you of you militant queers reading this and looking for something to be offended by can call me a coward all the way to the bank because I am debt-free, bitch!

I saved my parents from being bigots. If I had told them the truth, I don't think my life today would be dramatically different. At the time they thought they were doing the right thing; my mother probably still thinks she did the right thing. Society and time would have embarrassed them. When you are on the wrong side of history, I guess all you want to do is dig in and hold on for dear life. I saved them from making an ugly choice. They would have made that choice because of their own brainwashing, and ideas that are not even theirs. After twenty years of my parents protecting me and my future, now it was me, the child, protecting my parents from making a misstep on our future.

> "I take myself seriously. Therefore, you should take me seriously."
>
> – Chase Padgett

TINA IS A BONCH

As a child, I never went trick-or-treating because my family did not celebrate the "Devil's holiday". This of, course, was very frustrating to me because I wanted to do what all of the other kids were doing. Candy? Yeah, that's cool.... but for me, it was all about dressing up in a costume. I am sure if I was allowed to dress up, I would have had the best costumes as child, but we will never know. Halloween quickly became my favorite holiday as an adult. The first Halloween I was old enough to do what I wanted, I borrowed an idea from some former co-workers: I dressed up as my boss.

At that time, I was working at a corporate book store, which turned out to be the worst job I have ever had. In the beginning, there were a lot of really cool people (I am still friends with a handful of them today)—but, eventually, all the cool people left and then it really sucked! The reason working there was a prolonged suffering was my boss and arch nemesis, Tina. She was loud, obnoxious, peppy, nitpicky, a cougar—and she busted my balls every day. She would hide behind racks of CDs, listening to my conversations with customers, and as soon as those conversations were over she would pounce on me for talking too much, too slowly, or not selling something. Tina was a manager who spent more time micromanaging me than actually working herself. She had it out for me ever since she was promoted to second in command. Number One, our general manager, Carla, resembled a Hippopotamus. She was a giant fag hag, and I was her favorite. All of these factors came together for the best Halloween revenge of all time.

Tina felt she could whittle me down to nothing so that I would bend over and just start taking her bullshit and she could engineer a situation to fire me. A lot of times, attractive women are just used to manipulating men because men want to have sex with them. Gina, like many attractive women, went on autopilot when interacting with me; she either didn't know or constantly forgot that I didn't want to have sex with her; therefore all her flirty tricks didn't work to win me over.

That year the holiday fell on a Sunday, and a coworker threw a well-attended work party on Saturday night. My "Tina" costume for Halloween was a spot-on: perfect wig, a Goodwill business suit, a name tag, tights, heels, and attitude. Everyone knew exactly who I was and it was a whole evening full of lewd jokes at Tina's expense. Now the best part of my revenge was the mandatory store meeting before we opened the next morning. It being Halloween, naturally, I came dressed as Tina. Because of the party the night before I had some runs in my tights and, in general, Jay-Tina was looking a bit haggard. It was well received by everyone... except Tina. A man in a dress is funny, but a man in a dress as specific women and nailing it was comic gold. Every picked-on employee had a good ol' laugh with me at Gina's expense. Even the staff member Tina was having an affair with—and who was obligated to be on her side—gave a small chuckle.

She complained to Carla right away how it was unacceptable, disrespectful, and I was blatantly making fun of her (all of which were completely true). However, since Carla was a dumb, straight person who cared about gay rights, she mistakenly interpreted my costume as some kind of drag-equality thing. The hippopotamus told Tina, "He is not making fun of you; you're his inspiration, like Madonna or Cher."

This was the juiciest moment of revenge. The only person who could have put me in my place and stopped my freight train of Tina comeuppance was Carla, the general manager, who was too stupid to see it. Because of the power of Halloween, the Devil's holiday, I was able to pay back Gina by prancing around as her all day at work. Ladylike decorum was not followed and by the end of the day, I even had customers laughing along at my method acting.

After that incident, she came after me hard, but again being smarter and slyer, I always stayed a few steps ahead of her. I was already winning the war but my crushing victory came when I got a new job making the same (or possibly more) money than her. I curse you with the handles on all your grocery bags breaking. Hahaha.

SOCCER STORY

I play on a gay soccer team. I have for a while. We are in the lowest division of indoor recreational soccer. My team is very chill; we lose most games and that is okay. I don't like playing with people who believe it is really important to win. I don't like playing with teammates that tell you what to do from the sidelines or on the field. All of the teams we play in our division are equally chill, except for one.

This team was made up of "bro" guys, with a ringleader with a strong case of SMS (Small Man Syndrome). This guy reminded me of a bully from my high school who was short, rich, mildly attractive, and who thought he was hot shit. Clearly, the guy on the soccer team is not this bully, but to me, he was the same person. It is an interesting thing in life: if you are paying attention, you will notice that you meet the same people over and over again, but they are totally different people. When I encounter men with SMS, they usually will lay in on real thick because I am everything they are not. I am huge compared to them, usually one to two heads taller.

One day, a game was about to start and we were all in position and waiting for the ref to start the game. It was clear to me that there was an aggressive energy coming from the other team, mainly from SMS. He even boasted to a teammate and me: "If the ball comes to you or you, *I am going to charge you.*" Of course, the ball came to us. He charged my teammate, and then charged me, cheaply slamming into me. That was how the game started, and throughout the rest of the match, SMS continued to play dishonorably and aggressively.

I am not one to back down, especially in soccer. I am totally down for a rough game. People always underestimate how fast I am and how much bigger I am then... well, all of you. SMS kept slamming into me and I slammed him right back. This just provoked him, of course, because he was not physically able to move me. And I am fine with everything up until he made a comment so only I can hear, "I thought you were gay?" Meaning, how am I playing so well or so rough, because I am gay. How can a gay player be bigger, better, stronger than a straight player like him?

That comment got to me.

The game continued the ball went up the field, gets kicked around, and made its way back to me. Everything slowed down and SMS came for me. I very consciously decided what I was going to do and timed it perfectly. I faked a turn away towards my own goal and waited for the precise moment when SMS was just about to run into my back full force. Time slowed to a crawl. I knew what he was intending to do and I knew what he would expect me to do. I faked to run away from him but pivoted back on him with a grounded unmovable stance and my put my elbow right in line to clothesline his throat. Blinded by aggression, he fell for my fake completely. At the very last moment, right before the point where my elbow would have crushed his windpipe, he comprehended his mistake—but he had reached the point of no return and seized up in a desperate attempt to protect himself. If he had not seized up at the very last moment, 911 would have been called. He was completely clotheslined, landing with his shoulder blades on my foot and booty in the air. I promptly kicked him off my foot and stepped over his flopped-out body as I made my way off the field, getting a blue card. (Getting a blue card forces our team to play a man down, but that was preferable to getting a red card and being ejected from the whole game entirely. Truth be told, I should have been given a red card.)

He started screaming and freaking out. I said nothing. I was cool as a cucumber. He wouldn't stop yelling, and for that, he got a blue card too. Again, it was the same lashing out as a way to save face in the apparent loss of his masculinity. How could a gay man humiliate him so badly? How could a gay man almost kill him?

Sitting on the bench, my team captain turned to me and told me what I did was not okay, so I told him what was said to me. My captain wanted to say something to SMS, but I told him not to. I told him what SMS had done was wrong and that what I had done was wrong; we were even. The game finished without incident.

My captain later told me that despite what I had asked, he went ahead and spoke to the league, the other team's captain, and SMS himself. Apparently SMS did not deny the comment at all; in fact, he was very forthcoming. His response was that he had lost sleep over what had happened; he didn't like what he had done. SMS didn't know why he did that and didn't want to be the ugly person on the field that day or any day. Therefore, he was stepping away from soccer and was going to be spending some time working on himself.

It was then, right after hearing this, that I was glad I hadn't killed him. I am happy this dude had a realization that to make him want to better himself. I am happy I did something to stop homophobia and I wasn't just a gay doormat. It would have been nice if we won the game, but what can you do? I don't know how proud of myself I am for using violence to give this dude a giant wakeup call. I believe when "straight" men use homophobic slurs or are going out of their way to harass me or any gay person, that they are really are gay themselves[15]. Think about it: real straight dudes do not care about gay dudes; that just means there are fewer men that they have to compete with on the lady front. Oppressed and closeted "straight" dudes cope with their suppressed desires through hate speech. If I am saying these hateful words boisterously, then how could I really want to kiss that dude? I don't know. Could SMS have been using homophobia to assert himself as more of what our society tells men that they have to be? That could be just as true as well.

I am not going to deny that it felt good to scare SMS and knock him on his ass. I felt good to own that moment when there were hundreds of ugly moments and comments that were said to me where I did not stand my ground and take what is mine. The world has told me I am less than or that I don't deserve to be married, happy, normal, or whatever the fuck and that is bullshit. SMS thought he could walk all over me and he certainly doesn't think that anymore. It is really easy to breeze through life and not have courageous conversations with people who are spouting hate; I find it really easy to adopt the mentality to not waste my breath and those people with their outdated ideas will die off with them. We cannot do that. We cannot wait for hateful rhetoric to die off. We need to take what is ours because we have always been here, we are not going anywhere, and we deserve equality. Hopefully, we can educate without violence… but ya' know sometimes it feels really good to punch a Nazi?

---

[15] http://www.nytimes.com/2012/04/29/opinion/sunday/homophobic-maybe-youre-gay.html?_r=0Maybe

LAMY AMY FABEE

I live in a gigantic house and, therefore, have eight housemates. Since I have lived in my house for over eleven years now, I have had dozens of housemates. In the time living at my house I have lived with a woman named Amy Fabee, already a silly name. She turned out to be a giant piece of shit, so we nicknamed her "Lamy Amy Fabee" and this story is about her.

The landlord was planning to build a giant room in the basement of my house, big enough to rent to a couple. At the time of construction, I was preparing to leave for the summer to go on an Alaskan adventure. So on behalf of the house, I offered to sublet my room to a couple over the summer while the basement bedroom was being built. When I got back, I would return to my room and the couple would move into their new digs.

We found this great couple (or so we thought), Lamy Amy Fabee and her timid girlfriend. Newly relocated from Philadelphia to Portland, they were perfect and just what we were looking for. Lamy Amy Fabee had a small yipper-snapper dog. We never had a dog live with us before, but everything was so perfect and lesbionic, we said they could move in with the dog.

Two days before I left for Alaska, many things happened. The landlord decided he was not going to build the room in the basement. Lamy Amy Fabee and her girlfriend broke up. The girlfriend couldn't hack it and drove back to Philadelphia. Since Lamy Amy Fabee wanted to stay in Portland, she agreed to sublet my bedroom for the summer with her dog. I departed for Alaska and remained blissfully unaware of the disaster that ensued.

The first thing that happened was Lamy Amy Fabee acquired a second yipper-snapper puppy. And it turned out, Lamy Amy Fabee is a fantastically bad dog owner. She left her dogs locked up in the sun porch in the summer heat all day, every day. They pissed and shat everywhere, as well as, scratched the hell out of our solid wood door (original to the house). Now if you know me, then you know that my bedroom is a sanctuary of organization. In my absence, Lamy Amy Fabee turned my beautiful room into a disgusting lesbian clam jam. Sick, used tissues discarded off the side of the bed, dirty dishes of vegetarian wastes filled the corners, lesbian dog shit, dust, and lint covered dildos could be seen rolling about the floor. I was thankful to learn that one of my housemates cleaned it all up so I never had to see it. And lastly, she moved out in the middle of the night not paying her rent, utilities, and pet deposit. To this day, Lamy Amy Fabee still owes me $300.

When I returned home, I was made aware of this treachery by Lamy Amy Fabee. I decided I was going to run into her in public and she was going to wish she hadn't done that to me. Because I have a gift: if I wish to run into some one in public it will happen. I proclaimed to my housemates that I was going to run into Lamy Amy Fabee in public.

Three days later, I was driving down Division and I spot Lamy Amy Fabee walking into a 7-11. I pulled over. I had someone in the car with me, so I told them to hold on, as I had to do something. I walked into the 7-11. The guy at the counter and customers be damned, I say, "Lamy Amy Fabee. What's up? Rent? Utilities? Pet Deposit?" She looked like she saw a ghost. She ditched the Slurpee and walked out. I followed. She drove off and I was still yelling.

I went home to the housemates and we all had a good laugh at her expense. However, I decided that I was going to run into Lamy Amy Fabee in public again. Once was not enough.

Not even a week later, one of the best moments of my life happened: a true "Mighty Ducks" moment. It was a Tuesday evening around 6:30. I was playing a pick-up game of soccer at a park that happens to also be a popular dog park. It was prime soccer and dog park time. There were two full soccer games happening and an army of dog people. The soccer players were a bunch of bachelor dudes. The dog people were a whole bunch of young professionals who haven't had babies yet. And BOOM, I spotted Lamy Amy Fabee in the middle of the dog people.

I thought to myself that I have to do this; I was born to do this. I yell, "EVERYONE ON THIS FIELD!" Like magic everything stopped—soccer stopped, dogs stopped shitting—and everyone miraculously gave me their attention. "I want everyone on this field to know, that woman moved out in the middle of the night without paying rent and is a bad dog owner!" What happened next is going to sound unbelievable, but it's true. Immediately, all the soccer players cheered for me and all the dog people booed Lamy Amy Fabee as she walked off the field in shame.

People who move to Portland don't know this is the smallest town in America. Real Portlanders don't want to leave because we love the rain and we love running into each other everywhere. How stupid of Lamy Amy Fabee to think she could rip me off and continue to live in my city and never see me again. I have always valued public humiliation over any other form of discipline, and for Lamy Amy Fabee to underestimate that I would not run into her and I wouldn't say anything might be worth $300.

Now I am going to tell you another thing that is going to sound unbelievable, but it is true. In the year and a half it took Lamy Amy Fabee to move her pathetic ass back to Philadelphia, I must have ran into her at least a dozen times, and I did the same damn thing every time.

"There is no such thing as a free lunch."

It may not cost money, but it will cost you.

NIKAY

As soon as I retired from having a 9-to-5 job, I became a cater waiter. A friend of mine got me the job. She is a serving rock star and had over a decade experience in the service industry. Only on her reputation would someone like me—with zero service industry experience—be hired as a substitute cater waiter for the top catering company in Portland, OR.

I had no idea how much work catering is. It is hard-ass work. When you think it is done... nope, there are three more hours of work to do. Never think you are done when catering. I am just a substitute, so I only come into the event right before the guests do; the real catering crew was here hours before setting up. The kitchen, knowing what I know now, anyone who works in a kitchen works their fucking ass off and I tip my hat to them.

As hard as the work is, there is a part of me that loves it. Just buckle down and don't stop working until it is 100% done, or by the grace of God, you get cut early. Also, there is something about my boss that makes me want to work my ass off for her. There is something about her that I respect and want to impress. Of the bosses I have had, it is rare that I respect them, make regular eye contact with as a decent human being, let alone want to work hard for them. Beth has "it" and I would follow her into hell and back.

Part of working for a fancy catering company is you work at fancy parties. When you work a fancy party in Portland Oregon, then you will for certain work a Nikay event party. Portland's biggest corporation is Nikay and it really is a fluke; a company that size doesn't belong in little Beaverton, Oregon. Somehow it worked out that way, and we are stuck with them.

I did not know just how big a powerhouse Nikay is. I heard that you if you take all the shoe sales in the world from every shoe company in the world, from work boots to high heels, and added all the sales together, it wouldn't even be half of what Nike sells. This is just shoes we are talking about. Ever since the invention of the sneaker and Michael Jordan, Nikay has been king.

As someone who has seen Nikay's culture behind closed doors when they are letting their hair down and getting drunk at company parties, I can safely say that Nikay has a strong self-congratulating culture of waste. I once watched in horror at a Nikay conference where there was a "breakaway" for each team to get creative. Each team's table held a mountain of crafts: beads, string, markers, an entire box of clay... Being someone who ran after-school programs for years, I knew exactly how much each table was worth and how long it would last in a classroom. Each table had enough crafts supplies for an entire after school program for a whole school year.

The breakaway challenge was to put your Nikay heads together and make a new bridge for the Nikay Campus, and remember to think outside the box! That meant all these horrible Kool-Aid drinkers grabbed anything and everything that was not a craft supply: clean glasses, napkins, silverware, basically all our catering shit. I had a snooty Nikayette single me out to grab her empty microbrew bottles from the kitchen to add to her team's bridge. After telling her that we don't have any microbrews for her to not drink, she looked at me as if I was the only match for her bone marrow transplant and for some reason would not donate it to save her life.

Despite this serious setback to the 30 minutes of play time, each team made craft bridges which would make a second-grade teacher proud. A winner was announced and then all those craft supplies went straight into the trash. 100% of it was thrown away. The whole display was disgusting. It was the clay that got me. There are entire school districts in Portland where children have never and will never even touch clay because it is too expensive. And here Nikay is, wasting it for sport.

When I work for a Nikay party, I know I will be treated like a peasant. Everyone who works at Nikay is an asshole, which is a fact. Once I bussed the Nike Scotland table and was told, "That's a good lad"; I was 31 years old at the time. This treatment is part of what I like about the experience; it is important to be treated like shit every once in a while to remain humble.

I only have a problem when I have to witness Nikay assholes disrespect Beth. It happens every time. The Nikay party planners are of a lower Nikay caste and are treated just as poorly by the higher caste assholes arriving shortly. Even though they are bottom swoosh feeders, they are still Nikay employees, which means they are better than us. In order to boost their self-esteem, they hunt Beth down right before the real Nikay employees get there and find something to boss her around about. I watched a Nikay woman go on about a booze chaser not being accessible for twenty minutes, even though there was juice, coke, and soda water right in front of her fat face[16]. I really wanted to give her a wedgie in her ill-fitting Nikay jumper... but I didn't.

---

[16] There are very few fat Nikay employees.

At one particular party, I was scheduled to work the luge, something I had never done before. The luge at this party turned out to be a giant ice sculpture of Mt. Hood, which was taller than me by a few feet. On each side of the ice mountain, there were grooves carved into this sculpture for me to pour vodka shots down the ice and for it to go into a Nikay mouth hole. This was the spot of the party. Every Nikay bro and really hot Nikayette had to do the luge as a matter of solidarity. I poured expensive vodka down that ice sculpture for 6 hours. I am in hundreds of Bro photos I will never see[17].

The beauty of working the luge was witnessing the show of lemming after lemming embarrassing themselves all night. In order to take a shot correctly off of an ice luge, one has to humble oneself and adopt a lower and unflattering position while physically putting one's mouth on the ice and hold it much longer then you would think. To humble oneself is 100% a foreign concept for Nikay employees. It does not commute. And the beauty of this private show was any attempt to look cool, to save face, or attempt to have the vodka fall directly in their mouth the worse it was. How I poured and how much I poured of course was helpful or hurtful based on my discretion. Any rude request for, "Just a little, Bro," was absorbed by my smiling face and responded with half a pint of vodka shakenly poured in order to slosh up and down the sides of slowly melting ice luge. Clone after clone, I watched lesson after lesson of vodka going down shirts, soak shoulder pads, going in weaves, on faces, in beards, down chins, and in eye sockets. There was only one lady who did it correctly and was able to take the perfect ice luge shot, which by the time the vodka travels down the ice for that long it is refreshingly chilled and quite delicious. I was sure to tell her that she received top marks from me. As for the rest, they put on a quite the show and gave me, what I call, one of life's victories.

---

[17] #salesgoescoastal

Where Is Your Tray

One Nikay party I was catering, about 500 Nikay people show up wearing head-to-toe black. Everyone at this party is wearing black: fancy black, patterned black, fun black, and causal black. At the right moment, I found a Nikay employee who appeared to have just an ounce of resistance to the KoolAid. I approached and tactfully asked, "What is up with the black?" She responded in a slow and disdainful manner, "Those...were... the instructions, come to the party wearing black." I knew I chose the right robot to ask.

There were 500 people at this party with 99.9% participation to the instructions. The reason for wearing black, as is all Nikay instructions is conformity. You are only Nikay if you think like Nikay, which is think like a Nikay circuit breaker. And they were wearing BLACK. There were only 3 robots not wearing black. Two of them were wearing black, but it was a questionable pattern or checker print and I could tell they weren't Nike material.

Now the last robot not wearing black really shit the bed on this one. I am sure it was noted and showed up on a performance review. I don't know if this dude had a black sports jacket on earlier in the day, but he was wearing a white shirt with black tie, and black pants n' shoes. This just so happened to be the exact uniform of my catering company. This douche bag did not look like a robot but instead looked like the help.

The party started to wind down and another waiter and I bussed in tandem. In the courtyard, the douche bag sat alone at a far table creating the perfect opportunity. The other waiter and I hit his table, bussing used glassware and napkins onto our trays. I stopped what I was doing and made eye contact with this douche bag. He looked at me and I said, "Where is your tray?"

"...What?"

I slowly looked at him and drew his gaze the other waiter and then back at myself. I repeated with the condescension only a thespian can command: "Where is your tray?"

There was a moment of a blank caveman expression; then comprehension came. "Ahh, very funny." That was what he said, but what he meant was, "Don't compare me to a server! I work at Nikay!" [*Insert foot stomping and pouting here*]

I saw all the distasteful glances and heard all the superciliousness every time

I worked for those parties. But I always felt superior to them because, at their core, they were dim and easily manipulated. These people were (and, likely, still are) the scum of the earth because they have nothing of substance to their character. All they have is money. To be a cool person, you either have to make cool things or go see cool things. Nikay people are neither but have all the money in the world to just buy the pretense of 'coolness'.

Because it is not genuine, they are stuck in a cycle of searching and latching onto the next 'cool' thing with stacks of money weighing them down while completely blind. All these Nikay turds don't even know what they, as individuals, like. They only know they need to find it and they have the money to buy it. You could have all the possessions in the world, but in a fire, you wouldn't know which one to save.

RIBBON RACKS

When you pull up the image in your mind of any military uniform, you see that block of weird colors on the front of the uniform. Those are called ribbon racks and it turns out all those tiny rectangles of color mean something. (Who knew?) A ribbon rack is basically a soldier's resume represented in different ribbons folded in a very specific order and method. The US military will make the ribbon racks and provide a stipend for soldiers to pay for them and keep them up to date, but to update one's ribbon rack through the military takes forever. Another option is to go to a private company and there are only two civilian companies in our whole country for this service. One of those companies is in little Milwaukie, Oregon, just twenty-five minutes outside of Portland. I worked seasonally at that insane company because my buddy worked there, and I was thankful for this bizarre experience.

This company had around 40 full-time employees and ramping up towards December; they needed to double their staff with seasonal employees to keep up with the orders. This rush in business was due to the military balls happening in late December. Soldiers need to look dapper "AF" for those things or you might as well throw yourself off a bridge. The military, I am told, takes ribbon racks suicidality seriously.

Being a seasonal employee had the perk of no one investing in you in the slightest. Only two people knew my name: my trainer and my manager. Work meetings happened in front of us seasonal workers as if we didn't exist. Often I pulled out my ear buds and looked up to my surprise that the owner of the company was speaking to the group quite near me. A fire could happen in the building and no one would thing to alert the seasonal employees. But on the plus side, no one gave a shit and so there wasn't any small talk. How nice.

When someone made an order, that order went on a journey. First, the order was received and sent to the Pickers. The Pickers arrived at 6:00 AM and simply pulled all the supplies from the dozens of rows of raw materials, for the builders. The builders then made the order and sent it on to quality control. Quality control checked everything to either send it back to the builder to fix something and start again, or send it on to the second round of quality control. Once the second quality control signed off on the order being up to military-precision standards, they passed it on to shipping. Finally, shipping packaged and sent the order off to the customer wherever they are stationed. There are other departments too: metals, sewing, shadow boxes, customer service, ribbons, prepping supplies, T-shirt printing, and all the computer people who worked in the office. Every department in the warehouse got a few seasonal workers to help out with the rush. Of all the jobs a seasonal employee could be assigned to, I had the prestigious position of a builder.

Everyone was tested to see if they had the necessary crafting skills to make ribbon racks. Being the student of the arts and familiar with fine-point knives, superglue, and in general being a crafting boss-ass-bitch, I made the cut. Another buddy of mine did not make the cut and was stuck folding ribbons for metals all day. He folded four inches of cut ribbon for eight hours, every day. His trainer was a full-time employee, who worked there for 3 years. He asked his trainer since she had been there so long, had she done all the different jobs in the warehouse. Her response was, "Nope." This woman folded four inches of cut ribbon the same way, for eight hours a day, for three years. (This is the heights of Milwaukie, OR, people.)

I made twenty or so ribbon racks a day. From this experience, at a glance, I can tell what a soldier has done in the military so far: where their basic training was, if they had served in Iraq or Afghanistan, and if they had any special training or awards. You had to learn the names and meaning behind all of those perfectly wrapped and glued pieces of different colored/patterned ribbons in order to make a military-standard ribbon rack in the precise configuration of that soldier's service. This isn't just active service soldiers either; it was very common for older vets to order up a new ribbon rack[18]. Also, these things were not cheap. The average price of a ribbon rack was around $150 and 95% of the time a soldier would need to order two of the exact same ribbon rack for uniform and for dress uniform. Sometimes high ranking soldiers ordered their regular ribbon racks and then ordered a mini-ribbon rack. A mini-ribbon is the exact same thing, but one-quarter the size. Which means there was a whole hallway of all the mini ribbons and supplies needed to make those damn things. One day, I asked what they used the mini racks for and the answer was, "They don't use them for nothin'- maybe pin it to a teddy bear?" What the fuck?

The most remarkable fact about this business was the demographics of the employees. There were only three types of people who worked there (and this included seasonal employees.) Every person on the clock at that company was a member of one of the following three categories:

---

[18] All Vietnam ribbons and metals are as complicated as fuck. It was like performing surgery on a gerbil. Because of this job, I unfortunately hate all Vietnam vets as a side effect.

1. White Trash Riffraff

This group made up 60% of the workers. They lived in the area or lived far out in the boonies. Coming into Milwaukie, OR was the big city to these rural folks. They only worked there because of the location. A whiskey-tango worker once asked me how I was doing and I replied, "Oh, really using my Bachelor's degree today." That was the wrong thing to say to that person.

2. Ex-Military

Because of the tie-in to all things armed services, many workers got out of the military and didn't know what to do with themselves. They started working at this company because they speak the same language. The ex-military folks made up 20% of the workforce.

3. Queers

The last group was the most unexpected and, what I thought, would be the most out-of-place: *the queerest people on the planet*. I am not exaggerating. This 20% of the workforce were the gayest people I have ever been around. Super-sassy gay dudes, slinging sewing machines; an army of butch lesbians holding down the shipping department; and so many transgender people. It was awesome. Coming into this job, I was a bit on my guard as a gay person about coming into this rough and tumble environment. But not to worry: all these queer people were putting me to shame. In comparison, I could have easily been confused for either of the above groups.

To my bafflement, these three groups worked really well together. I don't know why or how this three-way slice of life worked so well—and believe me, I've put a lot of thought into it—but it did work and was a great team environment.

I was trained to be a builder and after about two weeks, I mastered the art form of ribbon racks and also impressed the worker bees with being also able to make mini-ribbon racks... then I started to get bored. I needed some excitement to get through the sometimes-ten-hour shifts (podcasts and music were not enough). Around my second week, I started eating marijuana eatables right before I clocked in at 6:00 AM. It was a whole new world.

This became my routine. I dug in deep for three or four weeks before the embarrassment of all the working class came down to me. Now I could do all the arts-and-crafts work, no problem, but the shelves were a whole other element of the warehouse I could never master. Just picture a windowless warehouse with at the least one hundred different shelves. They all mean something different and are a part of different interlocking systems with different departments giving and receiving with each other. Having mild dyslexia, there was something about what shelf to draw work from, and more importantly what shelf to put completed work on, that was bedeviling to me. Also, being a seasonal employee, I felt I was not being paid enough to learn everything correctly. And if I was going to die in a fire there, then fuck the shelves.

One morning, in particular, I put my finished ribbon rack on the wrong shelf and my manager came over to my station to point it out and be condescending, and show me the right shelf. Then I finished the next ribbon rack (perfectly) and was pretty sure what shelf to put it on. It was late morning, I was very much high at the moment—and my manager's berating was making me doubt myself even more. Do you ever have those moments where you tell or psych yourself up to do (or not do) that one thing, whatever it is, just don't do that? (*Wait, you're about to do that. No, stop doing that! Why are you doing that? Why can't I stop!?*) Well, that is what happened to me in that moment. I was so high and so scared of being scolded again. Walking with confidence to save face and conceal how high I was, I dropped off my work on the incorrect shelf and returned to my station. My manager swooped in like a clam jam and reprimanded me again.

Now, this manager was from the ex-military demographic and was repulsive to me. He was loud and disgusting. He belched at least once an hour from all the energy drinks or whatever slop he had just eaten. He swore in every sentence that came out of his pale mouth. Now, I am a comedian and love swearing and a casual work environment, but this was way too much, even for me.

"Oh, Jesus Fucking Christ! We're fucking out of the Military Defense Fucking ribbons. Shit!"

Even I am thinking, "Wow, pump the brakes dude. We are at work. And while you're at it, stop burping in my ear. That is fucking disgusting, bro." I complained one day about this manager to my buddy, who got me the job, and he absentmindedly said, "Oh, don't worry about it. That is all for show. I mean, he transitioned, what, three years ago now..."

Mic drop.

I was shocked.

This wasn't an ex-military man; this was a transgender man. All of this revolting bravado was all a gender performance. I would never have known my manager's personal business or history, which makes sense because he was a real dude after all. But I definitely was floored. My buddy felt horrible he had accidentally outed his co-worker and I felt bad that my manager thought he had to succumb to these nauseating lows in order to be seen as manly.

Third ribbon rack was done and ready to be shelved. Now I was really in my head and spinning on where the correct shelf was. Just like before, but this time in slow motion, I lifted my head high and walked to the totally erroneous shelf and my manager popped up like a slimy lizard bursting out of a used up reptile egg to catch me in the act. He was perplexed. He tried to contain his anger and looked at me like I was the dumbest person in all of Milwaukie, OR. At that moment, which was the apex of my marijuana eatable, I was the highest I would be all day. So in that moment, I might have been the dumbest person in Milwaukie, OR. Just like how I "didn't" know his secret, he didn't know mine.

That was a bad day. I went home and for the first time in my life, I questioned whether I was making mistakes because I was high or because of my mild dyslexia/shelf-learning laziness. It was so confusing because I was such a professional high person... but was I? I decided I had to stop eating marijuana eatables before work. No more!

The next day at work *sucked*. I still made mistakes and I still had a confusing time with the shelves. So I decided the following day I would rather look like the dumbest person in Milwaukie, OR than not be high for this piece-of-shit job. Play on playet.

"My time is not for sale today."

— Jose Guadarrama Torrés

Jobs are just jobs. It is crucial that the modern adult know that sometimes there are more important things or events than jobs or money, and in that situation, your precious time, your talent, and your energy is not for sale.

WORK SCHMERK

Everyone has to go to work (Well, mostly everyone[19].) Who has to go to work this week? Yeah... All of us. It sucks. We all have to work. Jobs can be fun and some of my best friends have been ex-coworkers. But practically, we have to go to work because of money. We have to sell our time to someone else for money. And we have to have money for rent, for bills, and for fancy new jeans.

But the problem is, in life (and particularly at house parties), people will ask the question, "So what do you do?"

We are trained to answer that gigantic question with what we do for work, what we do for money. Of all the things that we do with our lives, of all the things that we could say that we do. I do theater. I do arts and crafts. I play soccer. I could say my job is playing soccer. But instead we answer with what we do for money. And that defines who we are at that house party, in just one sentence.

"What do you do?"

"I work at Ross."

At that house party all you are is the guy who works at Ross. Nobody knows that you are really good at ballet or that you are really good at Netflix. You're just the guy who works at Ross.

I think we should answer that question with what our passion is. If you don't have a passion, then you need to get one. There are people whose passion is their work and they get paid to do it. That's the dream: getting paid to do what you love. They knew what they wanted to "do" and worked very hard to get there. Becoming a judge does not happen overnight. Med school's no picnic. You don't get to build the Golden Gate Bridge until you've done the St. John's Bridge first. Those people are living the dream. Those are the people I respect. That is the person I want to be.

There's nothing wrong with working a job that is just a job, to support your life, family, or passions. In America we have a flawed mentality that what we want should just come easily. It's an only-child mentality. I've finally learned that it's not going to happen overnight. It hasn't even happened for me yet; it's happening, but it hasn't happened. Getting to my life's work took a whole bunch of jobs. And here are some of them.

---

[19] Excluding those real housewives.

GROSS OUT

My first job when I was fourteen was as a soccer referee for children, and I was very bad at it. Every game it was always both teams doing all kinds of things wrong. But since one team was always crushing the other, I would only make calls on the team who was winning. Parents hated that. I only ref'd one season.

My second job when I was sixteen years old was at the Gresham Gross Out, commonly referred to as the Gross Out. In my interview, my boss, a very small woman named Jill, right before hiring me, looked down at my resume and said, "You spelled referee wrong." Oops.

I don't know if ya'll are familiar with Gross Out, but Gross-Outs are always a circus. A Russian, food-stamp circus. Just to give you some context, one of the floor managers I had was called Meth-head Mike. Meth-head Mike had a very active meth addiction and dental problems, both of which did not affect his work. In fact, he was very productive. In his own right, he was living his dream.

One day, Meth-Head Mike was facing the diaper section. One of our patrons had opened a bushel of diapers, taken one out, and replaced it with the soiled diaper. Poor Meth-head Mike reached over the stack and somehow his hand went right into the hole and directly into the used diaper. He pulled out his hand back to find four poop-covered fingers. These kinds of events were super common. I learned it was okay at Gross-Out to be a functional meth addict as long as you did a good job. And also, you could end up with poop fingers at any moment.

This was the best high school job I could have asked for. The owners and the managers were awesome. My main manager was named Debi and she was cool as hell. I told her my favorite band was Led Zeppelin and her response was, "I saw Led Zeppelin in the 70's. There was acid going through the crowd. And Jay, it was the good stuff."

I loved Debi. I could go to her with anything and she would give me the best advice, because it was always *real* advice. All of the adults in my life at the time (my parents and my teachers) were never "real" with me, and I could smell how fake they were: *"Maybe you should get along with your other parent? The rules at your high school are there for a reason. You shouldn't retaliate when someone does something unkind to you."*

But not Debi. I came to Debi one day and I said, "Debi… man, there is this guy at school who I just hate. He TP'd my parent's house. I've done a couple things to get back at him but I need to do something better. I just got get him good."

She advised me: "Jay, what you need to do is call up a gravel company and order a COD."

"What's that?"

"A Cash-On Delivery order of a whole truck load of gravel in his name, to be delivered to his parent's house at 7:00 AM in the morning. And if you really want to get him, make it a truckload of sand."

As you now know, it worked and it was AWESOME! Thank you, Debi! See, that is a good boss; someone in charge and can give you direction on the job, but who is going to be real with you off-the-clock, person-to-person, and give you real advice.

There's something about being in the same situation with your coworkers that can breed two things: great friendships or horrible blood enemies. In some of my worst jobs, I made the best friends. At Gross Out, I was hired at the same time as a whole crew of other guys from different high schools. We only knew each other through work, and so there were no personas to follow us. We all ended up working there throughout our high school years. We became very good friends. I would even be bold enough to say we became brothers.

Right before we all graduated, one of my Gross Out brothers, Bryan Burtch, unexpectedly died of heart failure. This was the first person in my life who died who meant something to me. It was so sudden. We all knew this job and working together was not going to last forever. We were all about to move on, but not Bryan.

His picture was framed and hung up in the store. That's it. Now no one knows who he was. He was just some guy who worked there and died. And that is all he was; he worked here and died. But he was so much more than that job. He was my friend.

HORDERS

After working at Gross Out for three and half years, I saved every penny and traveled Europe for a whole summer. It felt great to work hard and reap the rewards of that work by traveling. When I got back from Europe, I finished out the summer working with 'religious' kids at a Christian extreme-sports camp. The camp did this evil thing where they would put commercials on MTV in the surrounding area that asked, "Do you like dirt biking, skate boarding, paint ball? What about wake boarding? Then come on out to camp!"

The commercials would say nothing about God or that this was a Christian camp. All these (not-so-poor) poor saps had no idea that it was a little bit extreme sports and a WHOLE LOT OF BIBLE.

I got this job through my youth pastor, who was best friends with the camp director; it was his way of trying to "save" me. Though part of my job was to run a Bible study in my cabin and at this point in my life, I was definitely *not* a Christian. Usually my Bible study would start off innocent enough, and then a kid would say something stupid like, "Evolution doesn't work cause of the Bible."

And I would say, "Okay cabin, think about this: what if God was the one who got the ball rolling on evolution in order to create the universe and the rest is just a guessing game?"

A cacophony, "Oooh, I never thought of that. That makes sense. I am now an atheist."

Excellent.

I was not asked back.

Then I got a "real" job at Horders Books and Café. This store does not exist anymore. And now I owe all those campers an apology, because Horders closing down is clear evidence that God exists. She saw an abomination and smote it from the earth.

Horders was a lesson in that some places are cool to go to, but not cool to work at. I started there as a cashier and then I moved up to working in the café. The café at Horders was the only place I ever spit in someone's food. It was a coworker's soup and I only did it to get back at him for making me have a crush on him. Really, it was his fault. Then I became a bookseller, which really should have been called, "Helping stupid people find books." Here is what I learned at Horders: if you cannot find the book you want which is filed alphabetically, then you do not deserve to read it.

WELSH CARGO

For two and a half years, I worked at a bank that we will call 'Welsh Cargo.'

I worked in their cash vault, their *underground cash vault*. I know it doesn't look like it, but millions of dollars have passed through these hands. The general public has a misconception of what a million dollars looks like. In the movies, they have a million dollars in a brief case, which is complete bullshit. I know what a million dollars in any denomination looks like. A million dollars' worth of 20s is the size of a full Costco rolling cart. You know that Mormon family that is rolling up with three rolling carts at Costco? That is a million dollars in 5-dollar bills.

It really was bizarre to work in such a high-security environment. The only way to have access to the vault was to be interviewing for a job in the vault, be someone who already worked in the vault, or a kid on Bring Your Child to Work Day. Since I don't have a kid, I invited a family friend's kid to come see the vault. He now also knows what a million dollars looks like in any denomination, and is better for it. You're welcome! What was crazy was for Bring Your Child to Work Day, they would allocate $400 in 1's and make a money pit for the kids to play in. (I am totally joking, but that's what they should have done, right?)

My job at Welsh Cargo was focused on production. I had to be fast! In one shift, I had to count all the money from deposits from all around the city brought in by armored trucks. In an average night, I would count around $300,000. Every week I would count around $1.5 Million. In the two and a half years that I worked at Welsh Cargo, $195,000,000 passed through these hands. Basically, at the bank, you were only as good as how fast you were.

There was a woman who we called "the Queen." She could grab the most mishmash pile of money and compile it in one fluid movement. It would be completely pristine like you got from the mint that morning. She had worked in the vault for 14 years and was the fastest and most accurate money counter this side of the Mississippi. The Queen was a workhorse. She had a full-time nine-to-five job in the day, and then came to the vault and worked another five or six hours in the evening, and cleaned stables on the weekends for free room and board for her horses. The Queen worked hard, had a Camaro with 30 speeding tickets to prove it. I wanted to be as fast as the "the Queen."

What was so intense about working there was when I hit enter, that money went into an account. And one time I accidentally put extra $300,000 into a store's account called "Dome Hepot."

There are work slip-ups like not replacing the copier paper, and then there are ones that involve a lot of zeros and a misplaced comma.

Like many jobs, Welsh Cargo asked a lot of us. We had many emergency training in the vault and during one, we were told if there is a fire in the vault, the bank would like us to put all of the cash that we were working with safely in the inner vault before exiting the burning building. Yeah, right! In fact, I might take some! Also, we were told if the vault somehow was robbed, the bank would like us not to cooperate. Pfff! If someone is able to get in here to rob us, which is impossible, I am not going to not cooperate. In fact, I am going to tell the robber exactly what they need to know. I am not taking a bullet for Welsh Cargo.

With the exception of the Queen, the people who worked in the vault were wack-a-doodle shut-ins. They were mole people. They were all homeschooled freaks that the bank was too embarrassed to have in front of its customers. They were stuffed down in the basement forever like *Flowers in the Attic*. All these freaks worked in the vault forever: six years, fifteen years ... underground, no light, in the cash vault.

A woman who worked in the vault for 33 years was named Sandy. She worked in the vault forever but also bartended at the Eagles Lodge where she and her biker husband were members. She had bleached-blond hair, wore about twelve cheap gold rings, and was into the white-person-wearing-turquoise-Native-American-shit look. Are we getting a visual? She sounded like this:

"I am not done with my ten minutes. A real break is three cigarettes long. You gotta come down to the Eagles Lodge. We've got great drinks. You're only smoking two cigs right now? Smoke em' if you got em'. You got to come down to the Lodge. We're having a rummage sale. Smoke em' if you got em' right? How many hipsters does it take to bum a cigarette? Every fucking one. Hahahaha!"

There was a guy named Michael, who was my age but had been working at Welsh Cargo going on six years. As you can imagine, he actually was homeschooled, and he was indeed a freak. His diet consisted entirely of bread rolls from WinCo, Mountain Dew, and candy. That was it! He never ate a vegetable in his life. His Mike-and-Ikes would be carefully laid out at his work station in neat, color-coordinated rows. He ate so much candy that his teeth were just rotting out of his skull. And he truly was a mole person because he never saw the light of day. His underground shift would start at 3 PM. He would get off at 11 PM and head home (or to WinCo if he needed rolls), play video games all night long, sleep until 2:30 PM and go to work. The sun never touched his skin: a true vampire, but not cool, dangerous or sexy. He only wore dingy, blown-out, white under shirts. It was hard to discern shirt from skin. Are we getting a picture? If not, let me help you. This is a picture of Michael:

Michael was pretty bad, but his buddy, Gerry, was truly the most disgusting person I have ever met.

Gerry was adopted. He loved Costco sheet cake. He also lived with his parents. Those two sentences are synonymous with each other. A Gerry fact: at his adult birthday party, at his parents' house, there was a Costco sheet cake for the party and an entirely separate Costco sheet cake just for him. That is all Gerry wanted for his birthday. He wanted to see how long it would take him to eat nothing but that Costco sheet cake. It took him two days. For two days, only Costco sheet cake entered his weird, gangly body. Sick!

When he wasn't pounding down sheet cake, Gerry liked popcorn and he would eat it at work. Money is one of the filthiest things in the world. It is the dirtiest thing that you and 500,000 people touch every day. At the end of my shift, my fingers would be black. I would not touch anything until I washed my hands...twice! But Jared was having an oral germ popcorn party with millions of our dollars every week! Mole people!

When working in the vault, they were all freaks. Everyone was someone

Welsh Cargo brushed under the rug, away from the eyes of customers. Everyone was a freak... but then I was working there, too. Was I a freak? Was I a mole person? Luckily I was fired, so I knew I wasn't.

ALASKA

After I called out sick seven times in six months at Welsh Cargo, I was escorted out by security. I graduated college, and decided that I did not want to dread going into work. I wanted to get paid to do something I was good at, and would be different every day. So, I started working with kids. After so many years of counting the minutes on my shifts at these dumb jobs, I found a field where it was fun to go to work. I was a youth worker for seven years now. I am going to brag right now: I was really good at child management. It is my playful spirit that allows me to keep up kids. Plus, it is new and different every day, so the exact opposite of my other jobs.

I heard about a program in Alaska that would allow me to do youth work and travel all over the whole state at the same time. So for two summers I worked in the rural villages of Alaska, out in the bush, running day camps for kids. In the lower 48, we have the impression all of Alaska is rivers, mountains, forest, and bald eagles flying overhead. It is like that in about five percent of the state. But in the area of Alaska where I was working, there is nothing going on out there: just barren tundra, permafrost, and alcoholism. There are two things I now know about Alaska; everyone has a dog and everything is broken.

In the bush, the native Alaskans have their own way of saying things. They will say, "Are you take the Honda to town?" And a Honda is usually a four-wheeler. It doesn't matter what vehicle you have; it's called a 'Honda', even if it's a Chevy. It's like in the Deep South, where every drink called a coke.

To inquire about the time, people ask, "What time is it?" which is a stupid question because in the summer in Alaska it is always 4 o'clock. The sun is literally always at 4 o'clock. I was playing a game and the whole group of kids started to leave. When I asked where they were going, they said, "It's midnight, we gotta go."

"Midnight, shit, you're right! I thought it was 4 o'clock."

The most amazing things would happen and nobody would care. They would say, "That's so cheap." Once a Humpback whale came into the bay in one of the villages I was working at and I was blown away.

"Oh my God, a Humpback whale?!"

"Yeah, so?"

"It's right there!"

"So cheap."

"What? I think whales are cool."

"It's so cheap, it's not good."

Everything I thought was cool was "So cheap."

Alaska taught me not to be cocky. I used to consider myself a pretty good rock skipper—and I am, by lower-48 standards. But I should have known that skipping rocks is one of the ONLY things for kids to do in the bush of Alaska. And I was talking big one day and said, "Hey, I am the best at skipping rocks."

And this kid said to me, "Ya think you're a P.R.O.?"

"What's that?"

"Spell it out."

We went down to the river, and I took forever to pick out the perfectly shaped rock. I wound up and threw what I knew to be a truly impressive throw. It hit the water eight or nine times, then disappeared with a small splash sound. I brushed off my shoulders and gestured to my competitor for his turn.

This kid aimlessly picked up the closest rock—this oblong, dirty, brick of a rock—and threw it. The rock hit the water 15 times, traveled across land, broke a window, hit a man napping on a couch… my throw was so *cheap*.

RICH KIDS

After I worked with the kids in Alaska, I got back to Portland and worked with rich kids. I learned two things. Firstly, rich people are assholes and they have asshole children. These two kids, they were brothers and they were just little assholes. One of them kicked me in the shin with soccer cleats. And their dad who was the king of the assholes tried to tell me it was my fault his shitty kid kicked me. These kids were like Joffrey from *Game of*

Thrones: evil and never should have been born.

Their last name was Mor. So I would see the brothers at the beginning of school day and would say "Good MORning" (because I just had to). I didn't know those Joffrey's were even picking up on my clever pun. But they ambushed me by waiting until their asshole dad was standing right next to me, they said, "Jay, you know when you say good MORning to us, we don't like it."

"Oh, you don't like puns?" And I knew they did not know what that meant. Just try to explain what a pun is to a child, it is very difficult.

"Yeah, we don't like puns."

Then I waited until both the kids and the asshole dad were looking right at me and I said, "Okay, I promise I won't do it any Mor." It went right over their heads. So in my experience, rich people are assholes and MORons.

FAN MAIL

Part of what made it easy to go to work every day was that kids are funny. What they say was funny, but what they wrote was even better. I don't want to brag, but most of what I've gotten from kids was fan mail. I want to share with you some of the real drawings and letters I've received over the years.

"I will eat you space cupcake."

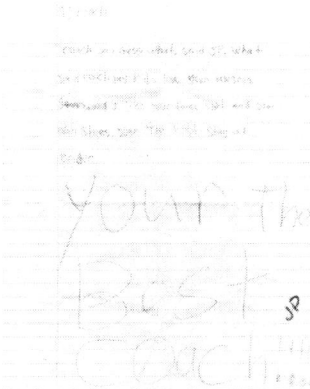

"Coach Jay guess what?"

"What?"

"Kids love your awesome games. And I like your fancy shirt and your clean shoes."

(I didn't think anyone noticed my clean shoes and fancy shirts.)

"Este es super Jay. Es muy fuerte."

Yo soy muy fuerte. I never got any fan mail at Horders…

Kids are also great at unintentional humor. Once I had my kids make posters for a food drive and without any influence from myself, a kid made this poster:

"May I have some food please?"

But that is not the full message of this poster, if you look carefully above the 'I,' this is what the poster really says

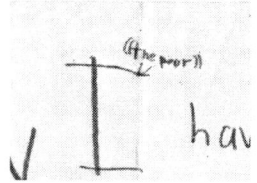

"May I, *the poor*, have some food please?"

What this poster was really saying was, "(aristocrat accent) Oh no, not me, I'm not hungry. I'm not poor; I am not a filthy peasant. I'm doing fine, living quite comfortably in fact." Furthermore, in the corner, there is a naked woman on her knees begging for food. Why?

Another thing that makes me laugh is that kids are the worst liars. I had two kids who insisted they did not have homework. So I said: "Oh, you don't have homework. Then go get a note from your teacher that says you don't have homework and I will let you do whatever you want."

They agreed, walked out of the room confidently, and came back in five minutes with this note.

"Dear Jay, --- and --- do not have homework. IT'S TRUE. Mrs. Thomas"

(BTW, this note on a piece of paper this size.)

"Why did Mrs. Thomas write this note on such a small piece of paper?"

"She just did…"

"But it's also written in pencil and this handwriting is really poor."

"She was in rush. I don't know."

"Well, it says it's true, so then it must true! Go do your fucking homework."

Believe it or not, I have received hate mail from a student. Our school was doing a student post office where they could send each other letters. The second year of the post office, I accidentally forget to send a letter to one of my favorite students. And on the last day I received this letter and was unable to reply.

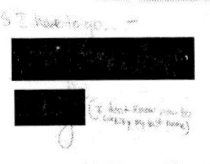

"Well, Well, Well Mr. Flewelling, I haven't received not one tiny, itsy-bitsy letter from you during this WHOLE post office weeks!!! I'm so MAD! How could you do that to me! Your [sic] so mean. (Not including the part that I bailed on you at SUN.) But that gives you no reason for you not to write one! Oh...I remember the ugly Trent days where we wrote each other about how ugly Trent was... (Or still is) (I hope). Yes, I looked up your last name in the phone book... don't get mad... Hey! Wait NO! That's MY job already! Well seriously you can't write me back because today's the last Post Office day so... Well I guess I have to go... (I don't know how to cursify my last name.)"

I think she will make a good manager someday.

GETTING FIRED/PLAYJERKS

Then I got this letter:

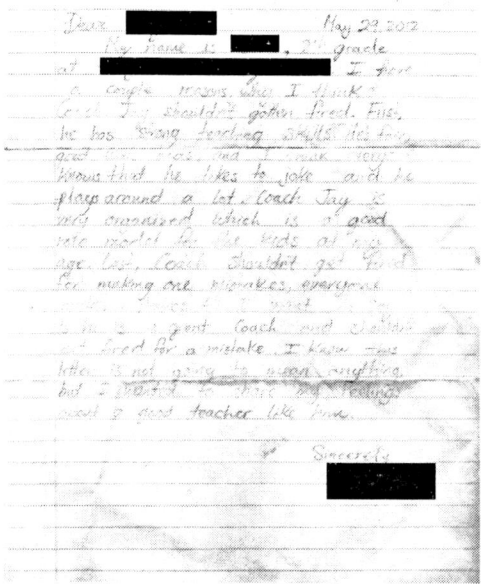

"Dear Playjerks, My name is ---, 8th grader at my school. I have a couple reasons why I think Coach Jay shouldn't have gotten fired. First, he has strong teaching skills. He's fair, good with kids, and I think everyone knows he likes to joke and play around a lot. Coach Jay is very organized which is a good role model for the kids at my age. Lastly, Coach shouldn't get fired for making one mistake. Everyone makes mistakes. All I want to say is he is a great coach and shouldn't get fired. I know this letter is not going to mean anything but I wanted to share my feelings about a good teacher like him. Sincerely, ---."

Once again, I got fired. This time, getting fired didn't feel right. It was a horrible feeling to be let go from a job that I had put so much of myself into. It was a horrible feeling to be called on my day off and told not to go to work tomorrow because I was under investigation. It was a horrible feeling to work at an elementary school and be under investigation.

I know what you're all thinking, and NO, I am not a predator. For three days I was under investigation and I didn't know why. My principal didn't know why. No one at my school knew why. Who does that? Ya know who does that: Frank Underwood. That's some House of Cards shit. Turns out, I was under investigation for not being respectful by putting my foot in front of a door that was being shut in my face by the 4th grade teacher who didn't like me, recess, or fun. (May that 4th grade teacher burn in Hell.)

I was never able to go back to my school to say goodbye and explain to the community I helped build why I wasn't going to be there anymore. But I was fired on a Monday. I had a job interview on Wednesday and I had a new better job the following Monday. So take that Playjerks! I washed my hands of them.

And I washed my hands of a day job ever being an identity for me again. At that point in my life, I had not started performing. Playjerks was my sole focus. It took getting fired in such a terrible way for me to realize that Playjerks was not my work. Getting fired pushed me to pursue my real passion: performing. My job doesn't define me – my *work* defines me. Comedy and my passion for performing; *my work* helped me heal from that traumatic job experience.

Playjerks was the last day job I put my blood, sweat and tears into. Having it unjustly taken from me taught me a lesson. There are jobs and then there is work; those are two different things. Work is the effort you put into something. I work to be a better person. I work to be a person who flosses their teeth and makes their bed in the morning. THAT takes effort. It takes no effort to default to the negative. It takes work—hard work—to remain positive and to flourish.

A job is something we all have to do. It can suck. It can be tolerable. It can be awesome. But your job is just a means to accomplish the real work that is important to you. I defy the notion and the dangerous mentality that your job is your identity. Your job is not who you are. You are not the guy who works at Gross-Out. You are not the guy who helps someone find books that are alphabetical order. And you're definitely not the guy who takes a bullet for Welsh Cargo. Those are just jobs. You are a painter. You are a writer. You are an athlete. You are an inventor. You are a mother, or family man … or maybe you really are just a great TV watcher.

If I have to have a job, then I want a job that doesn't destroy my body, or a job I don't loathe going to every day, or a job where the people above me don't respect me. I don't need to make a million dollars to do work that's important to me. Because that work is being Jay Flewelling. The work is being true to yourself. I work on being Jay Flewelling every day and I love it. And I put it to you to work on you. Your job? Job Shmob. I'll work on me. If you work on you, then let's hang out sometime.

"So? Sew your pants."

Anytime you hear someone say, "So," respond with, "So? Sew your pants." It will change your life.

WHEN WORLDS COLLIDE

Growing up I always wanted to be the favorite. I wanted to be my youth pastor's and teacher's favorite, and I never was. Plain as day, I could see who their favorites were and it was not me. I tried to decipher what the "it factor" was but I could never figure out the math.

One summer, I took a babysitting job as a nanny. I had been a nanny before and I was good at it. But this particular job I encountered the most powerful force in nature: nearly identical twin 1st grade boys. Never in my life had I worked that hard. Never in my life have I received that amount of attention from strangers. It wasn't me people were looking at; it was the twins. It was outstanding how many double-takes happened just walking around. People would come right up and start talking to the twins. I imagine that it was akin to people touching a pregnant lady's belly without asking.

99% of the time people were super positive. It was unreal. They were doted on. People told them they were cute, they were precious, they were adorable, they got attention for just walking next to each other. I would take them to get ice cream and not be charged. I took them to the arcade and the staff were following us around bumping the machines and making 1,000 tickets and prizes fall out. They were in a bubble; they were the center of the universe and I was just an accessory to them. I had a twinge of jealousy towards them because I wanted to be everyone's favorite when I was a kid and here they were, in reality, everyone's favorite, just for being born with someone who looks like you. Every time I tried to point out a teachable moment or hold them accountable for something, a stranger would come right up and give them a free elephant ear. Damnit!

One day I took them to Mt. Tabor Park. We ended up not at the main playground on the top, but at the small weird one on the side of the volcanic cinder cone. It appeared that we were all alone and had it to ourselves. And they ran up to the playground and just before making contact with play structure, they stop dead in their tracks. Hidden up until that moment was another set of twins: same age, the same level of cuteness, same adorable matching outfits. All four twins were completely freaked out! Time stood still. It was grid lock. Eight eye balls were locked on each other. They could not look away. Their hands would absentmindedly search for the next monkey bar. They could not process what they were seeing. It was complete brain warp. Does not compute. I went over to the mother and asked, "Are you seeing this?" And she said, "Yeah, I don't think they have ever seen other twins before." Apparently, my twins haven't either. I remember thinking it was odd that we were all alone. In a sea of attention, this Twilight Zone moment would happen with only me and the other mom to witness.

The twins never spoke to each other. They silently circled around the playground twice and my twins just took off. They gave up. I had to go catch up and they were shell shocked. It was like their super power had just been taken away. I let them walk in silence for a while to soak it all in, secretly loving the cruel lesson life just handed them.

There is a moment in everyone's life that you realize that you are not that special. It's the moment that you realize that you are not the only twins in the world and that is okay. It may not feel good, but that moment is important to creating a well-grounded person. It happened to me. It happened to those twins. It happened to all of us[20].

---

[20] There is a certain type of person from a nanny's perspective who has never had that moment and that person is called ...an only child.

HAMBURGER-EATING CHAMPION

I was informed, via being on the Burgerville e-mail list, about a Burgerville hamburger eating contest at my favorite and closest Burgerville location. Naturally, I was determined to enter and to win. I love Burgerville and I can eat a lot, so this contest was designed for my specific skillsets. For those who may not know, Burgerville is a fast-food burger chain only in the NW part of our fat country. They buy all of their food from local fat farmers and if you order a fat egg, they crack it open right then and there. All of their wrappings, napkins, and straws are biodegradable. All of their food is delicious and I could eat there every day and some weeks it gets close to that. Secondly, I can eat a lot of food in one sitting. There are so many people who will boost that they can eat a lot and it is all a show. In my case, I have to eat a lot and I can't stop eating until I am at capacity. To look at me, my ferocious need to stuff my face is not obvious, but witnessing one meal with me will change your gracious and dainty perceptions of me. Once a high school teacher of mine who was stunned by the speed that I ate, pulled me aside afterward with the concern only a mandatory reporter can command and asked me "Jay, is everything was alright at home? Are you getting everything that you need?"

I arrived at Burgerville an hour before the contest is supposed to start. The contest was part of an all-day Burgerville birthday celebration. The parking lot was filled with promotional booths for local businesses and there were music and general hoopla going on. After talking to three different managers, I finally found the one in charge of the contest. He told me that he might not have a spot for me. I gave him 'the eye' and he said, "I'll see what I can do." Since I was there, I decided to sit down in the lonely acupuncture booth in the parking lot and made friends with the lonely acupuncturist (are all acupuncturists lonely? Seems like it). Her booth was next to the Welsh Cargo booth, which was just as lonely with two bright-eyed, bored team members. I chewed the fat with the three of them while checking out my competition. There were eight competitors in this contest, with only four of them being noteworthy: a hipster, an old Asian man, an Elvis impersonator in full costume, and a roller derby lezzy and her lezzy posse. Lesbians always travel with a crew. It is lesbian law that you must run into one of your many exes every week—or, better yet, stay friends with them and continue borrowing clothes.

Now Hipster wasn't a threat, merely an annoyance as all hipsters are. He was in the contest because he was legitimately hungry and the contest was free. He was forthcoming with this information and believed that it was his ticket to win. All hipsters are fucking stupid, constantly proclaiming the most idiotic statements with the air that they are the smartest people on God's green earth. This guy was no exception. He had a crew too because all hipsters travel in packs with fanny packs.

The rumor had it Old Asian Guy, who did not speak English very well and relied on his family to interpret for him, was a winner of a taco-eating contest once upon a time. He was the competitor that I was most afraid of. Sometimes old people can eat a lot of food.

Elvis was quite the fun character to share the binge-eating stage with. He was lively and fully "on" way before the contest even started. But sadly his food eating abilities didn't hold a candle compared to me and would have really disappointed the King on his dismal performance. Maybe if it was a fried-banana-and-peanut-butter-sandwich-eating contest, his blue suede eating shoes might have put a little binge in his step...but not today.

Roller Derby Lezzy was talking big. Her girlfriend filmed this whole thing and went around conducting interviews with Roller Derby Lezy and her competitors, myself included. In most competitions, I usually play it cool and see what happens, but this was the first time that I was balls-to-the-wall cocky. In my interview, I proclaimed I am going to win this thing without breaking a sweat.

All the competitors took a seat at a long table as the hamburgers were brought out, and we awaited the start of the contest. I hoped they were going to be cheeseburgers, but no; they were just plain, dried-out hamburgers. Maybe they would have the Burgerville's famous sauce on them, but nope. They served to us cold, dry, and an hour (or so) old, like a burnt maxi pad. Each contestant selected an official burger counter to stand behind us to make sure we didn't cheat and count each burger we consumed. I selected one of the lonely Welsh Cargo team members. He was a fancy fellow. We had ten minutes to eat as many burgers as possible and with that, we were off.

In the beginning, I was patient because I had ten minutes and the tortoise always wins (we tortoises all know that). On my fifth burger, my competitors started to slow down. The hipster blew his load by his fourth but who didn't see that coming? At my seventh burger, I had a momentary feeling of doubt, but I quickly overcame the feeling with a quick inner pep-talk to myself from myself. While finishing my eighth burger, I left Old Asian Guy in the dust (these burnt maxi pads are not tacos!). It was just me and Roller Derby Lezzy approaching the ten-minute finish line. I wiped my mouth off from the eleventh burger I finished right as our leader called the time. Roller Derby Lezzy only got 9 burgers down.

I won a trophy, a keychain, a window sticker, a $25.00 Burgerville card, and a child-size T-shirt—as well as the glory! I also made Roller Derby Lezzy's crew do a reluctant and defeated post-contest interview with the Lezzy, Elvis, and myself. She didn't want to, but I made her. All in all, it was a great moment in my life.

PUSH N' SHOVE

I really do not like going bowling. As a youth worker, I have gone on so many field trips to bowling allies with kids, as well as with fellow youth workers for group bonding at the end of training. It is cheap, and most of my bosses have lacked any kind of creativity for something fun to do. Plus, it is disgusting: the white trash, the shoes, and your fingers going in the same holes as everyone else. If you have to go cheap with kids or coworkers, always go roller skating. I chaperoned for an eighth-grade graduation roller-skating field trip and it was one of the best days as a youth worker I have ever had.

This eighth-grade class was a bit of a tough crowd; there was a clear separation between the boys and the girls. The class was boy heavy and the culture of the guys in this class was being tough, lots of posturing, athletic, and a little mean. They all played basketball at recess and took it very seriously. For the most part, they were pretty good at it as well. It was hard for me to get them to lighten up and just have fun. The girls in the class were not as tough, but sort of blah. One of the most blah girls in this class was named Melissa. She was new to the school coming into the eighth grade, quiet, and was struggling with the recent loss of her younger sister. Being a wallflower put her on my 'blah' list, but after roller skating, she became one of the most important and inspiring students I have ever worked with.

It was Eighth Grade Day and we had a whole day of off-campus fun planned for the soon-to-be high-schoolers. When it came to the roller skating portion, everyone put on their skates and began. And from the start, it was completely clear this was the first time every member of this class had ever put on roller skates. All of these tough guy eighth-graders were falling all over the rink and themselves—hundreds of times. It was just silliness. For me, the height of humor is people falling. I was cracking up. For as bad as they were, they stuck to it and even played a game of roller hockey.

Now there were three people who could skate and skate well: a fellow chaperone, myself, and Melissa, the quiet unassuming girl. While everyone was falling and collecting bruises, Melissa was soaring gracefully around the many human obstacles, be they be upright or laid out on the floor. The power shifted that hour from the strong and confident to the inconspicuous Melissa. She was glowing, self-assured, and empowered. It was inspiring. This was Melissa's moment. No one could deny she was fierce and she was victorious. I could see months of being overlooked melt away. Her private struggle of losing her sister wasn't over, but this moment of being the best at something everyone is struggling with gave her assurance to carry on.

After the roller hockey game, Melissa and I got a little bored, so I suggested we play a top secret game just between us. The game was we would skate up behind or near people and give them a lighthearted scare. Melissa, in her new found roller skating confidence, eagerly agreed to this game. Being an adult and a chaperone, as much as I wanted to, I had no intention to actually scare any students. But that was not the case for Melissa. She jumped right in to this game and was going for the Gold. Friend and enemy alike did not escape her confident approach and surprising off-balancing startles that were light enough to taken as a joke, but strong enough knock a rookie roller skater off their feet. I could barely keep up with her gusto because of my debilitating laughter. Although I should never have suggested this game, it turned out to be such a powerful moment to bear witness to Melissa's transformation in to someone confident, someone who is self-assured, and someone who was winning. I'd say it is worth a few (dozen) bruises.

Not only did I enjoy the shit of bearing witness to Melissa's victory and mild bullying, but really it caused me to step back myself. I had been underestimating this girl. Countless times, I had not noted her as a student to invest in. It wasn't until I had seen her excel at roller skating and eagerly jump into a dark game of scare the shaky legs, that she was even on my radar. How many students, how many people have I not given them the right amount of attention or respect? Not only did Melissa teach me to give everyone a chance and not underestimate them the way I had been so many times, but she also taught me to rise up like she did. No matter how down I am, no matter how many times I am told "no", I will have my roller-skating moment, damnit.

"Less is more."

- Ludwig Mies Van Der Rohe

NAKED JAY

Guest Chapter by Jonathan Hopp

One might argue that the measure of one's friendships could be determined by the number of photos displayed within a collaged frame. If meaningful relationships are the key to a happy life (and they are), then the number of close friends in your photo collage that hangs in the hallway may say a lot about you. Plus, if you have still managed to keep a collection of physical photos alongside those displayed on a screen, then your effort implies a deep care for people in your life.

A frame with three slots narrows it down to the most important people in your life, be it parents, spouses, or most likely, kids. Photos of a formal family gathering, a couple snapping a selfie, or a child awkwardly posing could easily be the fodder to fill all three without a moment's hesitation. Four to six slots are only mildly more ambitious, but could indicate you are well-rounded and possibly a bit modest when it comes to immortalizing the important friendships you have cultivated. These photos aren't necessarily family, but could represent an array of connections that you feel help define you as an integral part of something bigger. The lesser relationships that may not have made the cut are still nevertheless significant—but, let's face it, maybe you just didn't buy a big enough frame.

Six to eight slots seem standard, with a random smattering of those who you hold dear along with the few folks who were once friends but might have faded into the inevitable background of life. They may have moved too far away; they may have started a relationship of their own (and maybe included you in their own collaged frame), or they may have just simply become no more than a quality snapshot of a time gone, but not forgotten. Either way, six to eight is a solid demonstration of those you've kept special despite the ever changing landscape of life.

With eight to twelve slots, you have a wide range of quality friends that you have to make damn sure you remember who they all are and exactly what they looked like once. I hope that this sentiment is true, and I commend you for going out there and cultivating these relationships. I know that I don't have the energy, but good for you! Finally, there are those digital picture frames, which, despite technically being a part of the digital age, almost always seem to be gifts that you would give to a parent or significantly older relative.

In 2006, before all of these frames with varying slots were completely obsolete, my wife, Jess, and I had a six-to-eight sized frame. In it were photos of the following:

1. Our dog dressed in old woman's clothing, including one of those hats that has a tiny veil meant to conceal the top half of your face.

2. A couple from Halloween past dressed as classy vampires, complete with flowing velvet robes and ironically high and stiff collars.

3. A couple of snapshots of friends we grew up with that had moved cross-country when we did and stayed.

4. A photo of myself dressed as Nicolas Cage in *Raising Arizona*, complete with pantyhose and Huggies.

5. A wedding photo that combined two male friends, one sitting coyly in the other's lap and both with trademark smiles.

6. And finally, the following gem:

JAY FLEWELLING

This is Jay and he is naked.

The story behind this photo centers around a camping trip Jay took with some friends of his. Upon waking early one morning, this gaggle of post-high-school, pre-college coeds decided unanimously that it was the absolute perfect morning to skinny dip. The sun was already nearing its apex, and it had warmed considerably to the point where it made the most sense to become naked and immerse said naked bodies in the frigid water. A round of snickering and encouraging phrases like, "Let's do this!" was all it seemingly took to get spirits motivated and heartbeats racing.

The water was always cold, and if beer commercials have taught us anything (and they have), we know that mountain water is the coldest and most refreshing water in the world. Jay, being the one to exude the most excitement over any quality idea, and also being the one known best for his follow through, initiated the disrobing with vigor and passion. With eyes fixated on the crystal-clear water, clothes were tossed behind in a flurry and Jay, naked as the day he met the world (but with considerably less hair), rushed to the edge of the water, poised to plunge. However, in a moment of hesitation, Jay turned, expecting to see his group of cohorts as equally thrilled and as equally naked sprinting towards the glistening pool at the edge of the rapid water. Instead, every friend sat in their same position by the fire, fully clothed, staring at him in disbelief and embarrassment. "Ummmm, yeah, we don't really want to *do* that," they said. Awkwardness hung in the air like the smoke of a morning fire pit attempting to burn through the wet timber. It was at this moment that he heard a camera go *click*.

My wife, upon hearing this story, instantly demanded Jay relinquish this photo so that it may bring joy to our picture frame. Being the generous friend he always had been, Jay followed through in its delivery. And so, this would become the story Jess and I would tell friends, family, and neighbors when they would notice this unusual snapshot amidst all the others within those six to eight slots. Inevitably eyes would always be drawn to that naked guy, and the story would be told again and again, with zest and laughter for the better part of two years. And so, like many tales once told, this particular gem became a legend of forgotten lore, a reminent that occasionally surfaced before sinking back into the depths of our collective memories.

A few weeks ago, Jay approached me and asked me to write an anecdotal piece for his book that would be "my Jay story." I was at once flattered and honored, but later my mind somehow went completely blank. The past fifteen years of knowing Jay were becoming a random assortment of hilarious and touching happenings that were suddenly difficult to weave into a single narrative. I put off writing, assuming something big would come to me, but sadly, nothing surfaced in my mind. Jay is such an amazing person and we have had years of good quality times—but damnit, where had they scampered off to? It was then that my wife brought up the memory of the very naked Jay photo and I knew I had to find it.

As I dug through our collection of a decade's worth of images, I reflected on the many people that have come and gone in my life: how I felt about them, what I loved about them, and how I missed some of them so dearly. Naturally, in my fervent search I found other pictures of Jay as well: Jay nailing it as Dr. Frank-N-Furter for Halloween; Jay in the woods, using an axe to cut slices of gourmet cheese; Jay mid-jump off a rock into a pool of water; Jay making his famous kale salad with a purposefully and comically stern look on his face. And finally, there was the photo in question: even more glorious than I remembered.

Jay asked how the piece was going the other day and I told him that it was going great. He inquired subtly about the contents of my writing, and I, always being the one to want to spill the beans about everything, couldn't contain the excitement and blurted out the entire theme. Jay listened intently and when I had given him the rundown, chuckled for a few moments, and said the following:

"Hmmm, that sounds awesome, but *I don't remember that at all.*"

Well Jay, one of our six-to-eight, now you won't ever forget.

"The early bird gets the worm but the second mouse gets the cheese."

Some of the best opportunities I had in my career was because someone better than me didn't show up and I was available as their 2nd or... 3rd choice.

TO EVERYONE I SPAM

There are a lot of people I spam about my comedy shows over and over again with about the same frequency as Donald Trump doing something embarrassing. Most of you I don't know, a good chunk of you are internet friends, and the last chunk is people I know and love.

To all the people who enjoy being spammed with all my comedy shows, I want to say: thank you for supporting me. Being a part of the laughter is something we all need in these troubling times. I also want to let you know that to all the people who do not enjoy being spammed, this open letter is for you.

1. I cannot stop spamming you. The ticketing service I use (and love) pulls a report from my e-mail to send out invites to my shows, meaning any e-mail that my e-mail has touched in the cold, cold night or any e-mail that has touched my e-mail in the cold, cold night is on that CVS report. It turns an e-mail list of 300+ invites from my contacts into a list of 1,200+ invites going out. So you can see why I cannot not do that. If you are upset, you really should be upset at the person(s) who did not blind copy your e-mail when sending out a mass e-mail that touched my e-mail in the cold, cold night.

2. Before you get mad at me, I also expect you to get mad at the big corporations first. (You know: the ones that Bernie Sanders is fighting against.) They are spamming you just like me, but 10,000 times worse, like all those Nigerian princes. Don't pick on the little guy; think like Bernie, and fight the MAN!

3. I am retired now. I don't have a day job anymore and it is GREAT! But it also means that comedy is my livelihood. In a way, spamming you is my new job.

4. Since I don't care and I am NOT going to stop spamming you, I have come up with a few calls-to-action that might help you out:

- You could just delete the e-mail without opening it. If you see my name, just delete it. I know, I know: that is a lot of work to delete one e-mail every time Donald Trump is a disgrace to the world. For example, if you are reading this sentence…you didn't have to. You could have turned the page. If you are about to go postal right now, stop reading this letter, close this book, and take a break. All that is going to be hard work, so be sure to take it easy for the rest of the day.

- Or, if you are still reading, one way to make yourself feel like you are the change you want to see in the world, would be to buy all the tickets to my show. Yep, buy every last ticket without using a promo code (cheapskate) so that no one will show up except the other opening improv teams. The show will just be another improv show of improvisers watching improvisers, as it should be.

- Or, this is going to sound unorthodox but… maybe… I don't know… You should just come to the show and have a good time? Sounds crazy, I know, but I this is probably your best option.

- The shows that I promote are not just some little thing that I am doing with my free time. Comedy is my life's work. It is my passion. It is my crack and I take my crack addiction very seriously. I put on a good show and if you want me to stop spamming you…(gulp) I will, if you come to one of my show first. If you need a free ticket or two, let me know and I will get you on the list. Not to toot my own horn, but if come to my show, you'll have a good time and afterward, I am pretty sure I hear you say, "Thank you, Jay, for stuffing my sweet little inbox full of spam. Never stop!"

You're welcome.

POOP

Poop is sick, but it is a fact of human existence. Everyone farts and poops, and everyone has thought they were going to fart and shat their pants. That has definitely happened to me. I generally think poop in all forms is fucking sick, and seek to avoid interacting with it. But, being a human, it is next to impossible.

For example, when I was going to a joke of a Christian elementary school, my sassy, eccentric frenemy, Sarah, came up to me on the playground and said, "Don't go over there and play with those rocks." In the far corner of the playground were three rocks stacked on top of each. Her enticing reverse psychology and the formation of the rocks indicating to my childhood mind, this was buried treasure and Sarah just doesn't want me to have it. Sarah was a crazy bitch in first grade and her very comment alone evoked me to defy her. I tore over to the stacked rocks and furiously began digging, my fingers were spread wide, raking though the pebbles that made up the ground cover on our playground. Before I could stop my arms from making those last three or four fatal swipes in the pebbles, I realized that I was thrashing though a giant pile of orange dog shit. In between each of my six-year-old fingers were clumps of warm, watery, canine feces; as if I had been kneading the dough of some would be pumpkin bread with my grandma. Right as I became fully aware of this horrifying discovery was Sarah's cue to wisp over and taunt me, bask in her victory, and flitter away like a gypsy. She did all of those things.

All of these stories are my stories where I failed to void to have an interaction with poop.

I started smoking pot in high school and I never stopped. I had some friends who wanted to smoke pot for the first time and their parents were going to be gone for the weekend. We got to together at their house and made a giant make shift pipe out of a one-gallon grape juice jug and some tin foil. Once the construction on the "pipe" was completed, we went outside to the patio to smoke. Now at that moment in time, my parents, without any real evidence, suspected I was smoking weed, and proclaimed they were going to test me for drugs "*sometime*." Looking back on that idle threat as an adult, it seems so ridiculous that I can't believe I fell for it. With the imaginary drug test looming over my head, I decided to make to the responsible choice and not smoke our shitty high school weed with all of my friends. On the patio there was me, my best friend, Taylor, Breecee Fleecee, Nate, and his younger brother, Brian.

On the patio, the grape jug went around once and there was the usual coughing that accompanies weed smoking. After taking the first hit of weed in his life, the younger and somewhat fruity brother, Brandon, wandered off unnoticed to the corner of the patio. The second round of grape juice went around and when it came to Brian's turn is when the collective noticed his absence from the circle. He was immediately found in his new location on the edge of cement in the corner of the patio where he has just taken a dump on the lawn. Pants down, boxers down, just taking a shit.

There was a moment of bewildered silence as the grape jug ember burned unattended. In this moment we were all in shock as to why this was happening. Everyone was on the moon and thus ensued a good twenty minutes of laughing our asses off. Brian was stuck standing there, continuing to shit and pleading for toilet paper, which all of us were incapable of retrieving due to a true laughing attack. This was his house and after the fact he had no explanation as why he didn't just go inside in the first place. The show continued, because he then buried his own shit/toilet paper, unaided, which took an absurd amount of time due to intoxication and crowd of hecklers.

As well as being a pot smoker in high school, I was also a Christian. I was heavily involved in my church's youth group and went on several church retreats. I was very afraid of coming home high, interacting with my parents and being caught. For me, church retreats were the best and safest times to smoke weed, because I wouldn't have to go home. Growing up in this church, I had years of being a weirdo to the whole congregation, so when I was stoned out of my mind and being a freak, nobody thought anything of it. On the last church retreat that I went on, Taylor and I had brought Ex-Lax chocolate to feed unsuspecting people. This was a prank we had long talked about doing, and now was the time.

The Ex-Lax chocolate bar had twelve squares and an adult was only supposed to eat one or two at the most. We got a couple of people to eat a square or two on the bus out to the beach, but this story takes place on the second night of the retreat. These were the early days of me smoking, and I was pretty sketched out by the time Tim walked my way. Tim was popular, good-looking, somewhat of a hot shot, and super dumb. This spider just caught a fly. We didn't really know each other that well, but I kind of started walking with him and casually offered him some chocolate. He ate two squares right away without stopping to notice "Ex-Lax" imprinted in every square of chocolate. That was when I decided to go for the Gold with this idiot and offered him the rest of the bar, wrapper and all. Tom walked to the other corner of the field under a light and ate the whole bar of Ex-Lax chocolate as I watched.

Fast forward several hours later... Taylor and I came upon bustling commotion at one of the boy's bathrooms. Apparently, Jaren, a frequently picked on underclassman, was being chased by a mob, and tried to find refuge in one of the boys' bathrooms. The mob followed and noticed that there were three or four plops of poop on the floor leading to the stall Jaren was cowering in. The mob, Taylor, and I all erupted into laughter and started yelling, "Jaren pooped on the floor!" This proclamation followed Jaren for the rest of his high school career largely to my doing. The best thing about it was that it wasn't his poop at all; it was that poor sap, Tim, who didn't make it to the toilet fast enough an hour or so earlier.

The next morning, I was still a little sketchy from the night before and I was in trouble. Big trouble. My church's youth group was so big that we had three youth pastors. The main youth pastor, Sam, I absolutely hated. I guess Tim spent all night shitting and puking and looked like a skeleton in pajamas this morning. Sam wanted to send me home but the other two cool pastors stuck up for me under the condition that I apologize to Tim (and Sam, the main youth pastor, for some reason). I immediately decided to not apologize to Sam, because, well... *fuck him*. I had to apologize to Tim on my youth pastors' orders, but also because I genuinely felt really bad that I had essentially poisoned him. But Tim was being a real dick about it and wouldn't let me apologize to him all day and that night. He finally was a person the next day and accepted my apology and called off his friends from threatening me. However, I found out on the bus ride home that Tim had slipped someone Ex-Lax chocolate about six months ago. Once I knew that, I was pissed I had succumbed to feeling bad and doubly pissed I apologized to that hypocrite.

.

I was hanging out with a new friend, Andrey, and I was going to go to his youth group just to check it out. I was dropped off at his house and we played around in his front yard. Unbeknownst to me, while playing around in the yard, I stepped in some day-old dog shit. Andrey was a car guy; his family just bought a brand new Honda, and his mom was taking us to youth group but he was going to be driving the car. We get in the car and right away Andrey said he smelled poop. The when I notice the dog shit on my own shoe. Because I didn't want to come forth and confess that it was I who defiled their brand new Honda. Instead I decided to stealthily flip over the carpet mat under my feet without anyone in the car noticing. Andrey again mentioned he could smell poop. The underside of the mat had sharp, black spikes. I proceeded to slyly scrape off the entire dog shit on my shoe using the black spikes, and when completed, I flipped it back over. I don't know why I did that, but I did it. We went to church and I never heard anything more about it.

.

The first house I lived in on my own I shared with a whole bunch of losers, one being a guy who I called Porno McGee because he worked at a porn shop. When looking for a job there are really two types of people: those that would even apply at a porn shop and then the rest of us. I lived with Porno McGee and he was a disgusting idiot from Olympia, WA. His bedroom was closest to the downstairs bathroom. One time, he offhandedly mentioned that I had pooped earlier that day, which I hadn't and told him so. His response was, "Oh, I thought I had everyone's poop smell memorized." *Sick*!

Next to the toilet in our bathroom was our washer/dryer, usually with a mountain of laundry on top. One day I was peeing and a suicidal sock tumbled down and landed in the toilet. I left the bathroom and announced to all my housemates, "There is a sock in the toilet. I am going right now to get a hanger and going to take care of it." In the seconds I went to get the hanger, Porno McGee went into the bathroom, peed on top of the floating sock, and then (of course) flushed the sock down the pipes. I came back and responded, "Did you not hear me? Did you not see the sock?" Both of these questions I might as well had asked the dog because of the blank stare I got from Porno McGee.

Now our household has to poop upstairs while waiting for a plumber to come and get the sock out of the downstairs bathroom, which took about a week. In the middle of that week, I was on the phone with a friend out of state and mid-conversation went to the bathroom. The conversation was good and I forgot all about the suicide sock and I sat down to take a dump. It wasn't until the whole thing was over that I remembered I couldn't flush. I was stuck. My friend still on the phone couldn't help me, so it was all up to me. I searched the bathroom for supplies and, amazingly enough, I was able to find two plastic gloves and a clear Tupperware with a lid. (I am still impressed that I was able to do this.) I safely got the shit out of the toilet and into the Tupperware, and secured the lid all while on the phone. It was an out-of-body experience, kind of like I was on the phone reporting the play-by-play of someone else disarming a bomb or something. But then what to do with the Tupperware? It was clear and my housemates were home, so I could not risk taking it through the house. Instead, I threw it out the bathroom window into our Buddhist neighbor's yard.

Our Buddhist neighbors had a baby, and were always coming over, asking us to be quiet or turn our music down. If this was the Middle Ages, that baby would be dead. So I figured they deserved a grown man's shit stuffed in a Tupperware container thrown in their yard.

In high school, I was a camp counselor for an outdoor school program which lasted one week at a time. Fun fact about me: I am not super into taking a dump in a foreign land and I avoid it if I can. Also, back then, I didn't take a duke every day. My poop period was irregular and I could hold it for a long time. So when I went to outdoor school, I had not gone for four days and it was getting to the point of crisis. All the campers were asleep, and we counselors would soon be dismissed to our cabins. My plan was to go to the public bathroom on my way back to my cabin because I knew this was going to be a crazy camp poop. But I totally forgot, went straight to my cabin, and was forced to use the fragile bathroom inside my cabin. This was probably the biggest shit I had ever taken in my life. There was a wizard's island of poop coming up out of the water. The first time I flushed the toilet, nothing happened; it didn't do a damn thing: not a sound, not any movement, nothing. The second time I flushed, all the water went right to the brim of the toilet bowl. I was scared it would overflow, so I shut the door of the bathroom and resolved to wake up before all of my campers and take care of it in the morning.

I awoke to my campers milling around on the ground below me. I watched, seemingly in slow motion, as kids were walking towards the bathroom and opened the door before I could stop him. As soon as the airlock seal of the bathroom door was broken, the smell flooded the cabin. It fucking reeked. A whole night of rotting shit smell jumped with glee into everyone's mouths. It was foul. All the kids went apeshit and I finally got down from the third bunk, looked in the bathroom just as I left it, closed the door, and turned around to face ten sixth-grade faces. I said, "I don't know who did this. I am not going to make that person come forward. I am just going to take care of it myself so that person is not embarrassed. So go about your business." While I lied to all of these children, they were *all* silently trying to figure out who defiled the bathroom, never once coming close to suspecting me, despite the impossibility of a child taking a shit that size and living to be embarrassed by it. I went to get a plunger, came back, plunged away, ignorantly thinking whatever inadequate time I spent plunging was enough and flush the toilet. Overflow. There was so much water that it is pouring out of the cabin on the outside.

I ran outside and the first staff member I find was a guy whose camp name was "Java." Java was a huge loser and just happened to be the staff member I didn't like the most. He came in, turned off the water, surveyed the bathroom, closed the door, and turned to face the entire cabin. Visibly angry, he turned to me and asked, "Who did this?" I said, "I have already spoken to that person and dealt with the situation." This angered him further, barked out to our cabin that this camp had weak plumbing, and ordered all of us to go about getting ready for the day while he cleaned up. He stormed into the bathroom shutting/slamming the door behind him. Not five minutes later, Java came out of the bathroom to address the cabin again, looking pretty pale. "I am going to need more ventilation, so everyone is going to have to clear out of this cabin and get ready in the public bathroom."

As we walked out, I was able to peek into the bathroom. I saw contaminated water all over the floor, an elephant-size shit in the toilet, and Java's puke all over the sink. It was a bad day to be Java and a good day to be me.

.

One morning, the basement of my house flooded. We called the landlord, a man in his early sixties, who we had a good relationship with. My landlord did not have any sons, only a daughter about my age. I am the son he never had; how we communicated was very similar to how I communicate and interact with my own father. The landlord came over and we went to down to the basement to investigate.

I was wearing Crocs and I tromped through the ankle-deep water in the basement with abandon. To my surprise, my landlord stepped right down into the water as well. Whereas I was wearing water shoes, he was wearing fancy white tennis shoes with socks and normal-length jeans. He didn't skip a beat and looked at me with confusion as to why I was looking at him.

We tromped and tromped and could not find the source of the water. The basement, being a hundred-year-old craftsman, was ever so slightly sloped to the center to the basement where there was a drain. The water certainly could not be coming up from the drain. No way! Mid-tromp, somewhere from the bowels of the giant house above us, a toilet flushed. In silence, we followed the sound moving around the many pipes and crescendo in a fresh turd being belched out of the drain on the floor. This whole time we had been splashing around a poop pool. Both of us immediately left the basement. I went straight to the shower and my landlord went home with wet-poop feet.

Over the next few days, while we waited for the plumber to arrive, the basement would flood and then recede all back down the drain several times a day. Because of this waning of the basement tides, lone turds would be left stranded about the basement like beached whales. My landlord dad tried to make me clean the basement, but I refused on the grounds that I wasn't qualified. (Take that, Dad!)

When the problem was fixed, my landlord called me up to report back. He said, "The plumber had a hell of a time because he pulled out over a hundred... Kotex's."

And then I said, "What is a Kotex?"

Silence.

"Ugh... it is a tampon."

I had never heard that word before. Now I understand. This was a lesson my landlord father had not signed up for, but he was damn sure going to teach his gay, tenant son about a Kotex. (Take that, Dad!)

So, why have I shown you all this filth? It's disgusting. I am sorry I went there after the whole book is almost over. This is probably the best book you've ever read in your life and now I've gone and shit the bed. If you didn't like this chapter and are not even reading this, know that the next and last chapter is the best one. I will win you back with the next chapter, I promise.

I shared my shittest moments with ya'll to unite us! We all poop and it is not such a big deal. Everyone has a good shit story. Everyone. Yes, we can laugh at ourselves because shit is funny. (Farts are funny too.)

Fart Freedom. Fart Any Where, Any Time. Join the revolution.

In a get-to-know-you game once, I asked a pretty white lady what her best fart story was and she kept saying that she didn't have one and couldn't think of anything. Bullshit. That pretty white lady should not have been weird or embarrassed by talking about her taking a huge steamy char, let alone pretty white lady farts. We all just need to own it—all of it—and rock it. There are two ways to win as a stripper: either you never tell anyone and just make tons of money, OR you own it like a rock star and make tons of money. Americans are so weird about going to the bathroom, nudity, and breast feeding. These are all normal things. Everyone poops, nudity is not always sexual (sometimes is just a body), and everyone was a baby who had a mom once. Why be weird or uncomfortable about these things? It is not necessarily an American thing. It is the culture of "NO" telling us to feel embarrassed and feel bad about our bodies. The world tells us, people tell us, and we police ourselves.

STOP. Get over it.

There are all those noble and fancy reasons to get into butt stuff. But there are also these less-noble reasons and shameless product placements as to why I took you to the water closet in this chapter:

The Potty Squatty

Get into it, people. We are not designed to give birth to poop in a sitting position. One of the many reasons taking a shit in the woods is so nice is because your body is in a squatting position. When we squat, everything is in line, and gravity is also pitching in (high five).

The Tushy

The bidet toilet is 1,000% essential if you don't want to be a heathen. Now that I have got my Tushy, I will never go back. The only reason America doesn't have bidets is that we didn't want to be European in how we take a dump. Well, it turns out bidets are not a European thing; bidets are a not-having-shit-hanging-around-your-sweaty-taint kind of thing. It is like the placement of the letters on a keyboard. The placement of the letters on a modern day keyboard comes from the typewriter. Many first versions made sense, but people typed too fast for the technology, so they kept making alphabet placements in more and more difficult positions. The now standard version is the most difficult version, designed to slow the typist down. So is the toilet-paper method which is entrusted to clean your asshole. All you are doing is mashing poop in and around your skin in the warmest and clammiest part of your body. Yum.

Get yourself a Tushy and blast that shit off of you. Go easy on those dials the first time for sure because you don't want to hurt your sweet, sweet cherry. There is a learning curve, but when you have mastered it, truly, you will never go back.

MOUNTAIN LAKE JAKE

For a very brief period, I worked at a Christian "extreme sports" summer camp called Mountain Lake. If you have never worked at a summer camp before, you would not know, as a camp counselor, you are paid nothing and worked to death. There is an acceptation in labor laws when it comes to camp employees because a counselor works sixteen hours a day for pennies. Sleep deprivation is just a part of the gig. So when it comes time to put your cabin to bed and its lights out, there is nothing more that you want than to go to sleep. More often than not, the campers don't want to go to sleep; "lights out" means "party time".

This is what I experienced my first week of camp. Each week at camp was a different age group of campers and that week was elementary-aged kids. When it came to lights out, my cabin would not go to bed. My helper, who lived in the cabin with us, wanted to go to sleep and I wanted to go to sleep, but our campers would not let us. They were at camp. They were on vacation. This was party time. Lights-out was a time for shenanigans, fart stories, and scary stories. As a responsible youth worker, I didn't allow scary stories because no matter how much they wanted it or if everyone said they wanted to hear them, I knew that there were some kids who didn't want to be scared and were too nervous to speak up. My cabin was obsessed scary stories, and one very specific scary story: "Mountain Lake Jake". Because this camp was called Mountain Lake and there was a lore of Mountain Lake Jake as the camp's local boogie man. Every night it was the same, "We are not going to bed! Tell us the Mountain Lake Jake story!"

I was raised a very strict Christian. I never went tick-or-treating. I never went camping. I never heard scary stories. Hannah Barbara Bible adventures were basically it for me. I had no reference point for anything that they were asking for. It got to the point where I had to ask other staff members, who were former campers and grew up to be staff: "What is Mountain Lake Jake?"

"Oh, it is the scary story of this camp."

"Yeah, but what is the story? I have never heard it before, and my campers want me to tell it BAD."

"Oh, there is no real story. You just make it up and use the name Mountain Lake Jake."

That night it was the same thing. My cabin wouldn't go to bed and wanted to hear the Mountain Lake Jake story.

I said, "Fine. You won't go to bed and you want to hear the story. Well, here we go."

I told them a story and it just sucked. It completely fell flat. It was not scary at all. I might as well have told them *Toy Story*. One camper even told me so: "That story sucks."

My story was so bad that the cabin felt I was placating them by not telling them the real Mountain Lake Jake story. Now they were even more indignant about hearing the story or they were never going to bed. Now I was pissed.

"Fine, you want to hear the real Mountain Lake Jake story? You won't go to bed. Fine. I am not supposed to tell you the real story but you made me. Let's do this."

So, not having any reference for scary camp stories, I just re-told The *Silence of the Lambs*, switching out Buffalo Bill for Mountain Lake Jake. And I went for the gold. I took my time and I spared no gory details. And I ended with: "Mountain Lake Jake is still out there, making skin suits out of campers at night, so don't get up and go the bathroom in the middle of the night, he is looking for a size 8 ... and you all are a size 8. The end." Boom. I went to sleep. I passed the fuck out. Dead to the world, sawing logs.

When I woke up the next morning, the first thing I noticed was that all of my campers were doubled up in the same bunk, asleep clutching each other in fear. It was like seeing the preserved ash bodies of Pompeii.

The second thing I noticed was: it smelled like piss. Multiple kids wet the bed on each other because there was no way in hell they were getting up to go the bathroom that night.

I felt horrible. I had accidentally scared the literal piss out of my cabin. What I didn't want to do, I had done. The good thing was for the rest of the week, everyone went to bed at lights out and nobody wanted to hear any scary stories. But I vowed never to tell scary stories again.

Fast forward to the end of the summer. It was the last week of camp and the age group of the campers was high school. This was the point in the summer where I was the most sleep-deprived, and this was the age group which required the most energy. I got a cabin from Hell. Because they were not really high schoolers; they were eighth-grade graduates. They were still riding on the high of being top dog. They had not gone through the crushing experience of being on the bottom again. (That freshman experience, I believe, is important for all people to have.) They all came from the same school and came to camp knowing each other and requested to be in the same cabin. The first thing they did was switch their names around so I never knew for certain all of their real names. (It's very difficult to control a child if you don't know their name.) They pulled other antics, like going through my stuff when I was away from the cabin. All of these kids sucked. I hated all of them but I was still determined to not tell scary stories.

It was the same story when it came to lights out. They were not going to bed. There was no way, no how. And they wanted to hear "Mountain Lake Jake". There was no way I was going to do that again. But each night they just would not go to bed. It was as if they all did a whole bunch of crack right before the lights went out. My resolve to not tell "Mountain Lake Jake" story got weaker and weaker as the week went on. Come Thursday night, I gave in.

"You won't go to bed; you want to hear the Mountain Lake Jake story? Well, here we go."

I started with *The Silence of the Lambs* version and it didn't take. They were not scared at all and one kid even said, "Isn't that *Silence of the Lambs?*"

No, no it's not. Again, they wanted the real Mountain Lake Jake story.

In that moment I got an idea and I decided to roll with it.

"Alright, you won't go to bed. You all want to hear the real story. Fine. I'm not supposed to tell you, but you win. The only place I can tell you this story is on the dirt bike trails. Get your flash light and your shoes on; we are going on a hike."

Half the cabin was gung-ho, the other half was losing faith.

This camp was on acres and acres of woods. The dirt bike trails were the most remote and the most wooded because the trails go through the woods. I didn't start telling the story until we were on the dirt bike trail. I began weaving a tale of Mountain Lake Jake, and this version had a heavy dose of dirt-bike influence. Mountain Lake Jake was a camper. He loved dirt bikes. He was bullied. Yadda yadda yadda, now he's a murderer who roams Mountain Lake on a dirt bike looking for his next victims. Late at night if you hear a lone dirt bike engine, it's Mountain Lake Jake on the hunt.

At this point, we were deep in the woods. It's dark and it's cold. The timid half of my cabin was scared and wanted to go back. The gung-ho half of the cabin was not scared but were close. One more gory detail and I had them... then we could turn around and finally go to bed. All of sudden, somewhere up ahead on the trail, a very clear sound stopped everyone in their tracks: a dirt bike engine.

The gung-ho half of my cabin was visibly shaken. A few members of the timid half of my cabin were crying. Honestly, I was scared too. My cabin was scared because of the story; I was not because I knew I made it up. I was terrified because I didn't know who was on a dirt bike deep in the woods in the middle of the night. I tried to make it seem like this is all part of my plan and I ordered us to turn around and head back to the cabin.

As we started to briskly walk back, it seemed as if the sound of the dirt bike engine was not only following us but gaining on us. My brisk walk turned into a light jog out of fear. I thought that whoever was on that dirt bike was going to turn this impromptu life lesson into *deliverance*. My helper was freaked out. Tears now entered the gung-ho half of my cabin. The timid half of my cabin was experiencing full-blown panic. The dirt bike engine was still there and I started running because I was now very scared. And I yell "Every man for himself!" I could not have planned this better. My whole cabin, including myself, was completely petrified out of their mind. I again accidentally scared my whole cabin and now myself. This cabin deserved it and I definitely deserved it as well.

We made it out of the bike trails and back to our cabin. I never found out who or what was on that dirt bike. I don't know how anyone could have pulled off a prank like that without word getting to me in the morning. But the two things for certain were:

1) There definitely was a dirt bike engine chasing us.

2) For the rest of the week, at lights out, my cabin went right to sleep.

"There are a lot of people who are good starters. There are not a lot of people who are good finishers."

Anyone can start anything. It is the determined and the hard worker that will finish what they start and not give up like a piece of shit.

THANK YOU (CONCLUSION)

Thank you for reading my book. I hope you enjoyed it and maybe some of you were inspired by my stories, experiences, and perspective. Visualize. Actualize. I am exceedingly proud of accomplishing this goal; I wrote a book. I am an author! That is huge. All of these stories are special to me and are a huge release to have them written down as if they might have drifted away if I didn't get them on paper. Some of these stories I love, think about and perform often. Some stories are very personal, vulnerable, and were hard to share. As the living legend, RuPaul advises: don't take it too seriously. Now that these stories are out there, please enjoy them and be kind. If you are not kind, just know I don't read comments. Your hate will fall to the wayside of the internet, and may you step in a puddle with a sock on forever and always.

For those of you who enjoyed Please Underestimate Me and were motivated by my stories, thank you. We are creatures of great possibilities and are usually only limited by ourselves. Do not let the culture of "no" stop you. Walk into every room as if you own it. Notice and collect every insult, negative slight, disdainful glance, and every statement from the world that is bringing you down, collect them like coins in a piggy bank. Know the more you are underestimated, the stronger and richer you actually are. It may not be today, it may not be tomorrow, but you are ready to cash in. We are all ready.

Thank you.

Jay Flewelling

<u>People I am grateful for:</u>

Krysta Drechsler
-
Kimberly Brady
Megan McGeorge
Jose Guadarrama Torrés
Jonathan Hopp
Jess Hopp
Marisa Latico
-
Keith Flewelling
Deborah Flewellingf
-

PLEASE UNDERESTIMATE ME

Caitlin Kunkel
Ken Wells
Eric Hedford
Andy Batt
Jake Trudell
Nicholas Wilson
Pierce Anderson
Jason Edward Davis
-

Jed Arkley
Craig McCarthy
Bill McKinley
Ashley Barton
Annie Rimmer Weeks
Savira Kambhu
David Alexander
Emma Weightman
Devlin Farmer
Jill Sughue
-

Jason Rouse
Scott Engdahl
Stephanie Cordell
Shareen Jacobs
Blake Wales
Rose Bonomo
Savira Kambu
-

Mortified
Susan Estes Danehy
Kevin Allison & RISK! Podcast
-

Specifically, I would like to not thank RACC for not funding this project two years in a row. BUT I would like to celebrate and THANK from the bottom of my heart the following people who did support this project and gave me a validation kick in the pants. Thank you:

Hugo Cordova
Byron LaDue n' Kathi Diamant
Marisa and Katie Latico
Elliot Matson
Barbara and Stephen McGeorge

Beth Parazette
The Shannon/O'Brien's

Lastly, a big THANK YOU to everyone who underestimated me. I wouldn't be where I am if it weren't for all you assholes!